Kierkegaard's Theological Sociology

Kierkegaard's Theological Sociology

Prophetic Fire for the Present Age

PAUL TYSON

CASCADE *Books* · Eugene, Oregon

KIERKEGAARD'S THEOLOGICAL SOCIOLOGY
Prophetic Fire for the Present Age

Cascade Books
An Imprint of Wipf and Stock Publishers
199 W. 8th Ave., Suite 3
Eugene, OR 97401

www.wipfandstock.com

PAPERBACK ISBN: 978-1-5326-4825-0
HARDCOVER ISBN: 978-1-5326-4826-7
EBOOK ISBN: 978-1-5326-4827-4

Cataloguing-in-Publication data:

Names: Tyson, Paul.

Title: Kierkegaard's theological sociology : prophetic fire for the present age / Paul Tyson.

Description: Eugene, OR: Cascade Books, 2019 | Includes bibliographical references.

Identifiers: ISBN 978-1-5326-4825-0 (paperback) | ISBN 978-1-5326-4826-7 (hardcover) | ISBN 978-1-5326-4827-4 (ebook)

Subjects: LCSH: Christianity and the social sciences—History of doctrines | Christian sociology | Kierkegaard, Søren,—1813–1855—Criticism and interpretation | Kierkegaard, Søren,—1813–1855 | Kierkegaard, Søren,—1813–1855—Ethics | Kierkegaard, Søren,—1813–1855—political and social views | Religion—Philosophy

Classification: BR115.S57 T97 2019 (paperback) | BR115.S57 (ebook)

Manufactured in the U.S.A.   03/28/19

With gratitude to John Milbank, the pioneer of twenty-first-century theological social theory, and a wonderful mentor. And with much appreciation for Gabriel Rossatti, Knut Alfsvåg, Jeffrey Hanson, Eric Austin Lee, John Betz, and Christopher Ben Simpson, all of whom are outstanding scholars of Kierkegaard and Hamann whom I am privileged to count among my academic friends.

Contents

Introduction

WORSHIP IS WHAT UNIFIES all communities. Yet worship is not a merely descriptive category, for worship (*worth*-ship) can be true or false as regards a proper valuing of the Good. Hence, it is the right worship of God that enables human flourishing for individuals within human communities. Consequently, idolatry—the wrong evaluation of ultimate value, the love of anything in the first place of worth that is not God—deforms communities and forms the individuals embedded within those communities in futility. For this reason, the study of the pathologies of society is the study of idolatry. Equally, ecclesiology—the study of what the church really is—is the study of the healthy human community.

Because communities are composed of individuals, and because no individual exists in isolation from the communities to which they belong, collectively situated worship is also central to each individual's human identity. The relationship between communities and individuals is a two-way street: communities form and define individuals, and individuals shape and compose communities. But thinking from the direction of the individual, the study of the common categories of psychological pathology[1] is also

---

1. This book is not concerned with what we now call psychological illness. By "common categories of psychological pathology" a Kierkegaardian perspective has in mind those aspects of human psychology that are considered both natural and normal to what St Paul calls the carnal man. For following St Paul, Kierkegaard sees the Old Adam's bondage to the elemental principles of the fallen world as persistent pathologies embedded in normative psychological dynamics. Here there is no necessary connection between

the study of idolatry, and soteriology—the study of how the individual is made right in their primary relation to their Creator—is the study of the healthy soul.

This does not mean that the church and individual Christians, in practice, define community and psychological health. Indeed, any concrete expression of the church is always going to struggle with idolatry, for this is what it means to be the church militant. There is no place for triumphal hubris in the militant church. Equally, no Christian can suppose that their own psyche is without persistent pathological bents toward disordered worship. We wait for the final purification of the last baptism before we are fully free of the Old Adam. Yet the church and Christians should be continuously struggling against their own tendency towards idolatry.

Kierkegaard was painfully aware that at some decisive historical junctures the struggle of the church against its own idolatry is almost hopelessly lost. At these points God raises up irritant messengers—unwelcome Socratic gadflies—to tell the idolatrous "house of God" that its witness to the world is fundamentally compromised and its own judgment is pending.[2]

All of the above seemed obvious to Kierkegaard when he wrote theologically framed studies of his own society, his own church, and his own soul. But this understanding of society and the soul does not seem obvious to many social scientists or psychologists today. It does not even seem obvious to many contemporary Christians.

---

that which is psychologically *normal* and socially normative and that which is psychologically and socially *healthy*. For example, Kierkegaard treats all the normal causes and dynamics of despair, anxiety, aestheticism, jealous, pride, unbelief, some forms of morality, the desires underpinning both seducing and seduction, etc., as theological pathologies of the unbelieving soul. Equally, Kierkegaard treats the normal levelling, competitive, and trivializing tendencies of the mass media as theological pathologies of the idolatrous community. On Kierkegaard's psychology, see this very helpful text: Evans, *Søren Kierkegaard's Christian Psychology*.

2. Kierkegaard saw himself as such an irritant. See Pérez-Álvarez, *A Vexing Gadfly*.

Introduction

I have written this short little book because I think Kierkegaard is right about worship and its defining relationship to the soul and society. This means I also think the central "classical" thrust of our methodologically materialist and non-theologically framed social sciences, and our likewise framed psychological sciences, are wrong. Badly wrong. If we are trying to understand human society and we have a fundamentally wrong conception of what constitutes the human soul, our social and human sciences are going to have a bizarrely abstract and point-missing quality to them, no matter how rigorous their empirical data and statistical analysis is. Worse still, the technologies of personal and societal manipulation that are produced by our spirit-excised human sciences may well be powerfully useful in shaping society in a *sub*-human manner. If there is a serious theoretical problem in the way we understand what it means to be human beings who live in communities, this will have more than merely theoretical implications in the application of what we take to be valid social scientific knowledge.

To work toward re-thinking the study of society in a theological register, this book aims to do two things. Firstly, I want to draw your attention to Kierkegaard's doxologically defined sociology as a wonderful example of how this penetrating way of thinking works. And I don't just want to show off Kierkegaard's exotic theological sociology, but I want to argue that *because* of his theological framework, he does sociology decisively better than the "classical" social scientific norm allows. Secondly, I want to play around with applying Kierkegaard's way of understanding society to our own context. It is my hope that once we get a clearer theological understanding about what it means to be social beings, we will be able to think more clearly about how our society actually works and what a discerning Christian response to the sociological needs of our times might look like.

I have written this book at a time when it is now possible to think as a social scientist and a theologian in ways that have been largely out of bounds in the social sciences since shortly after Kierkegaard's lifetime. Before embarking on that task, it is worth briefly situating Kierkegaard's thought in relation to the social sciences.

The text by Kierkegaard that this book will draw on is his *Two Ages*. As probably the first serious critique of the modern mass media, it remains a classic in the field. Arguably, it may even stand above the field as one of the most penetrating works of the past two centuries on what public opinion is and how it actually works. Indeed, in this book I will argue that *Two Ages* is enduringly insightful precisely *because* it understands social dynamics in the categories of worship. *Two Ages* is ideally suited to bring this out because in it Kierkegaard gives us a doxologically framed social analysis of Golden Age Denmark. By "doxological" I mean that his analysis is defined by a careful understanding of how "the logic of worship" plays itself out in various social settings.

However, Kierkegaard's *Two Ages*, written in the 1840s, signals a road not taken as the social sciences developed in the nineteenth century. As Kierkegaard writes, Karl Marx is lifting his critique of capitalist society into the air. Marx takes as his starting point the work of Ludwig Feuerbach, and turns Feuerbach's work into a thoroughgoing materialist critique of religion. Via this critical move Marx believes he is able to get at the real material practices of collective power that define—as he sees it—the concrete dynamics of social organization. In the modern discipline of sociology, Marx is counted as the first of the three great classical sociologists, with Durkheim and Weber being the other two.[3] Marx's metaphysical materialism is slightly softened by Weber and Durkheim, and in its place the functional materialism of methodological atheism becomes embedded in classical sociological method and interpretation. So after Marx, the main current of the emerging social sciences largely accepts methodological and interpretive norms

3. As a sociologist, I am greatly indebted to all three of the classical sociologists. They are giants in the field for good reasons. Yet Kierkegaard's way of combining careful social analysis with a theological interpretive lens sets him apart from the classical era of social scientific inquiry. The interpretive lens of overt materialism in Marx's case, and methodological atheism in Weber and Durkheim's case, is deeply problematic if human beings are in fact spiritual beings.

that exclude the kind of theologically framed social analysis that Kierkegaard pioneered. As a result, very few works of similar bearing to Kierkegaard's theological sociology gain anything like recognition within late-nineteenth- and twentieth-century social scientific scholarship. This does not mean that first-rate theologically framed social analysis was not being done,[4] just that this was largely done without the mainstream of social scientific thinking taking much notice of it. But things are changing now.

I did my doctorate in the sociology of knowledge in the 2000s. What made it possible for me to work within the social sciences from theological premises was the impact of a remarkable text by John Milbank titled *Theology and Social Theory*.[5] Milbank points out that secular modernity is itself a theological construct. From here it is clear that modern materialism is a culturally situated and (ironically) theologically generated interpretive lens, and that methodological atheism cannot be taken seriously as an objective truth discourse once the postmodern critiques of modernity are properly taken into consideration. Hence, we are in a position to radically re-think social theory, and to re-think social theory from theological warrants.

Broadly speaking, Milbank's work has been well received in the field of social theory. This has not been where opposition to Milbank's work has arisen. Indeed, it is various establishment elements within the *theologian's* guild that have taken a particular dislike to how Milbank upsets modern theological orthodoxies.[6]

---

4. See just two examples from the mid-twentieth century: Guardini, *The End of the Modern World*; Ellul, *The Technological Society*.

5. Milbank, *Theology and Social Theory*.

6. Nineteenth-century progressive thinking was both seeded and advanced by the powerful ways in which nineteenth-century German Protestant theologians were scientific, liberal, and modern. Theologians deeply shaped the rise of progressive and liberal social-reform movements. Yet equally, the conservative fundamentalist backlash against liberal theology and progressive politics in the early twentieth century was a deeply *modern* enterprise. Fundamentalists embraced a radically literalist biblical hermeneutic as a form of biblical positivism, and fundamentalist non-conformist Protestants were deeply committed to liberal political arrangements and modern middle-class entrepreneurialism (market liberalism). It is not surprising that *both* self-consciously modern

But in social theory itself, this field now usually understands that sociology cannot presume the automatic validity of materialist assumptions in its methodological and interpretive enterprises.[7] In this context, the "progressive" orthodoxies of classical sociology are no longer mandated.[8] It is now entirely possible for serious academics to do social science from theological warrants. This is possible in social scientific academic circles, but what about in theological and Christian circles? Could it be that theologians and Christians who are natives of the modern, scientific, and secular age are more resistant to thinking about society through a theological lens than are academic social scientists?

---

theologians indebted to liberal theology *and* self-consciously conservative fundamentalists indebted to liberal political and economic secularism should find John Milbank's theological critique of secular modernity distressing.

7. The norm of social scientific thinking is still situated within methodological atheism and reductive materialism, but this is now understood as just one particular methodological framework and interpretive lens, rather than the only valid methodological framework and the only true interpretive lens. At the level of social theory, the "progressive," twentieth-century reductive positivism of a stridently British atheist and American pragmatist bent has largely faded. What we are seeing emerge is a much more hermeneutically self-reflexive social scientific outlook. The subtleties of French genealogical and cultural theory and German interpretive philosophy have now strongly influenced the field. This is an outlook aware that culturally and narratively situated interpretative frames are radically inescapable when we seek to understand human society, particularly in the areas of religious studies and in the interpretation of meaning in any social context. See Josephson-Storm, *The Myth of Disenchantment*, for a fine example of this more self-reflexive contemporary social scientist.

8. This leads to the awkward situation where if a social theorist does not adhere to the methodological and interpretive orthodoxies defined by "progressive," nineteenth-century ideological commitments, they are likely to be labelled as a "conservative." This is ironic, for in fact progressive ideology is now the old and outmoded *conservative* establishment of yesterday's social sciences. Certainly the ongoing conservative vigor of social scientism remains a powerful force in the academy (and more so, in government policy and educational circles). This outlook has the superficial sheen of academic orthodoxy because the twentieth-century academy was indeed the first home of progressive liberal ideology. Even so, naïve positivism towards this ideology is now an intellectual embarrassment to serious social theorists.

Introduction

I am writing this book for lay Christians, clergy, and theologians who live within the late-modern life-world of liberal, Western, and secular consumerism. In this context, the social sciences are open to a theologically framed analysis of social dynamics, and yet Christians seem unaware that there is a ready niche here for us to fill. We should not be so shy, for the richness of the resources of our faith in understanding the human world are, if Kierkegaard's lead is anything to go by, profoundly illuminating. So let us not hide the light of a theological analysis of society under the bushel of sermons and theology books that never get outside of that bizarrely locked-up sphere designated for faith and the church by secular modernity. Let us explore how society looks when viewed through a theological lens.

PART ONE

Kierkegaard's Theological
Sociology

1

Sociology and Worship

WHAT IF COLLECTIVE PRACTICES of worship are the most basic orientation points within any given sociological life-world? Let's play with this thought a bit. Imagine we live in the ancient world, say in the time of Augustine of Hippo. To Saint Augustine it was obvious that the thing that distinguished the Christian way of life (what sociologists call a distinctive life-form) from the way of life normative to pagan Rome was *worship*. That is, Augustine thought that the first shared object of highest loyalty in pagan Rome was different to the first shared object of highest loyalty in the church. Here Augustine is following a basic New Testament insight where an innate doxological and praxiological[1] tension exists between the world and the kingdom of heaven.

In the *City of God*, Augustine argues that devotion to one's own glory is the first object of Greco-Roman pagan worship. An agonistic conception of self-love—as supported by shared cultic practices and a common set of values, power structures, and commonly known mythologies and meaning narratives—defined the

---

1. I will unpack this further below, but "doxology" refers to our understanding of what worship is and what it entails, and "praxeology" refers to our actual lived actions, our practices of life that embody the doctrines and theories that we believe.

pagan Roman life-form (the City of Man). In contrast, so Augustine maintained, a peaceable devotion to the glory of God—as expressed in the love of God first, then the love of neighbor as oneself—defined the common values, aims, and norms of the Christian life-form (the City of God). Taking matters of collective worship as basic to any given shared way of life, and taking those frameworks of common devotion to be intimately entangled in spiritual realities, Augustine then thinks about how Christians might live out a different mode of shared life to the world, that is yet for the true interests of the world (which is its conversion to right worship).[2]

I have asked you to think about the role of collective practices of worship in a "what if . . ." sort of way because, to the assumptions of secular modernity, such a notion is quaintly hypothetical. We, so we like to think, have removed worship from the public realm, and made it a matter of personal freedom. We like to think that we do not have any shared framework of common devotion defining public norms, for every individual is free to have whatever personal religious convictions they like. Worship, so we imagine, is structurally removed from the sphere of public life and common law that regulates our shared codes of right and wrong. Further, our social sciences are typically "methodologically atheistic" and treat all social phenomena materialistically. Religion itself is understood materialistically in what we might call the mainstream of modern secular university knowledge. Given that we think of religion as a private individual affair that should be held discrete from the public sphere, and given that our smart thinkers about society tend to assume at least a functional or methodological atheism, it would surprise me if you, like Augustine, thought worship was obviously the key issue defining sociological life-forms. But I think Augustine is right.

2. If you are interested in knowing more about Augustine's spiritually dynamic sociology, see Chanon Ross, *Gifts Glittering and Poisoned*. This is a beautifully written and accessible exposition of Augustine's understanding of the role of the spectacle and the arena in the ancient world. Ross then relates Augustine's insights to our own consumer and celebrity society. We will return to Augustine and Ross' text later in this book.

It only became an assumed and obvious truth to the norms of the modern social sciences that Augustine was wrong after the 1840s. The materialist critique of religion that blossomed in the mid-nineteenth century was particularly stimulated by two German thinkers, David Strauss, a theologian, and Ludwig Feuerbach, a philosopher. Strauss published *The Life of Jesus* in 1835 and George Elliot translated it into English in 1846. In this book Strauss argues that none of the miracles of the New Testament can be believed by scientifically minded people, so the real meaning of the life of Jesus is moral and mythic. Feuerbach published *The Essence of Christianity* in 1841 and this was also translated into English by George Eliot, in 1854. Feuerbach argues that humanity creates God in its own image. These theological and philosophical movements that purport to see through orthodox Christian belief do not just pop up out of nowhere. These trajectories are in deep continuity with aspects of eighteenth-century rationalist and empiricist thinking, and with the powerful intellectual influence of Kant and Hegel on the early to mid-nineteenth century. For whatever reason, the dam walls containing reductions of reasonable faith to scientific, moralistic, and political terms, and the social sensibilities containing the radical atheism of a growing cohort of intellectual elites burst in the 1840s. This is the context in which the social sciences as we now know them were born.

A combination of increasing secularism in Western Europe's intelligentsia and the manner in which rationalist and empiricist trends (often pioneered by historicist biblical scholars) found their intellectual fulfillment in materialist atheism, made the climate right for the bold new thinking of Karl Marx, the first of the three founding fathers of classical sociology. The other two—Émile Durkheim and Max Weber—pursue distinctive trajectories to Marx in notable areas, but the methodological atheism that got into the air in the 1840s never left the social sciences thereafter. Until, that is, recently.

The social theorist Bruno Latour's *We Have Never Been Modern* looks at the supposed demarcations between the meaningless pragmatic objectivity of a materialistic secular sphere and a private pluralism of subjective religious freedoms and moral value commitments and discovers that this cannot be true sociologically. That is, we are inherently social beings and the public and the private are always, in fact, integrated within any (even our) sociological life-form. The theologian John Milbank's *Theology and Social Theory* looks closely at modern secularism and discovers that this way of thinking and living has very deep theological roots going back to the fourteenth century. That is, modern secularism is itself a theologically embedded life-form. The anthropologist Talal Asad's *Formations of the Secular* unpacks the blind spots, unprovable assumptions, and political commitments of secularism—it is no methodologically neutral and objectivist way of seeing the world. Peter Berger's *The Descularization of the World* points out that the materialistic secularization thesis, which held that religion inevitably dies as societies progress, is simply empirically wrong. The theologian David Bentley Hart's *The Experience of God* points out that the conceptual grid through which modern materialist critiques of religion think about God and faith has no comprehension of how people of faith actually experience and theologically understand God.

Actually, the materialist critique of religion and the uncritically secularized view of society has always been deeply contested, before (Hamann), during (Kierkegaard), and after (Nietzsche) the 1840s. Even so, the 1840s were a switch point, a time at which it became culturally feasible to think of social scientific knowledge in secularized, functionally atheist, and materialist terms. One thinker who rejected that outlook entirely, and produced a theologically defined and doxologically centered sociology, was Søren Kierkegaard.

KIERKEGAARD, MARX, AND THE SOCIAL SCIENCES

As mentioned above, the 1840s were a remarkable decade in the history of Western civilization. In this decade we saw the sure-footed rise of a materialist conception of the social and human, sciences that ended up profoundly reframing the way we think about who we are, what the meaning and purpose of our lives is, and which practices of life are reasonable. This is the decade when the clarion call of progressive reform rings out, signaling the casting off of the shackles of all traditional norms, justifications, and power structures. Hereafter, no established way of life can be taken as sacrosanct. In the 1840s—after the Protestant Reformation, after the Scientific Revolution, after the French Revolution, and in the teeth of the Industrial Revolution—it now seemed clear that Western Christendom was coming to a decisive end. At this point, the tide in the affairs of men turned at its most fundamental level. From here the epistemic, metaphysical, and normative assumptions of the intellectual culture now flood away from Christianity, rather than being drawn towards a Christian vision of the highest good. Now—so progressive thinking maintained—all things were to be made new and better in the dawn of a genuinely scientific, egalitarian, and humanist future. Progressive optimism felt sure that it was only a matter of time until we all came to embrace a functionally atheist and pragmatically materialist form of individual and social realism.

Two of the greatest thinkers of the 1840s were Karl Marx and Søren Kierkegaard. Both read Feuerbach's groundbreaking *Essence of Christianity* with keen interest. With astonishing candor, Feuerbach argued that we humans create God in our own image. This is, on the one hand, a totally shocking rejection of mainstream religious conviction and doctrine. On the other hand, there is little in Feuerbach that was not already thought to be obvious in the high philosophy and radical theology of the German intelligentsia at that time. Feuerbach simply joins the dots between the Hegelian emergent political philosophy of Spirit and the type of historical biblical speculation made famous by David Strauss.

But Marx did not read Feuerbach as a good Hegelian. To Hegel, Spirit evolves in history through matter, but to Marx matter and time themselves are what produces Spirit. To Hegel, the emergence of his own German idealist philosophy is the emergence of creative Spirit itself. Marx turns this around so that matter creates thought, and material realities generate grand ideas—such as Spirit. The true meaning of emerging mind is entirely materialist for Marx, such that all ideas of transcendence are the product of human material reality, and there is no divine source that generates material man. To Marx, Feuerbach's work discloses religion as an entirely human construction, and this enables everyone to see what religion really is. After Feuerbach, no reasonable person—so Marx holds—can fail to grasp the freedom that is ours to make meaning and power suit our real needs and desires, without recourse to some non-existing god that we project upon an unreal transcendence. The sense of liberation and possibility is electric as Marx contemplates this situation.[3] From here Marx made the critique of religion the basis of all progressive critique. Traditional Christian categories were now inverted; transcendent divinity becomes an idolatrous false consciousness, and the worship of humanity becomes the only true piety. Now old loyalties are treated with fundamental suspicion. For the false consciousness of religion is not only delusional, but its real (that is material) meaning is the use that religious institutions and the individuals invested in those institutions put it to. The real purpose of religion is the perpetuation of the political and economic interests of established power and privilege, over the exploited masses. Class warfare is the foundational social reality, and religion is one epiphenomena of that war.

To Kierkegaard, Feuerbach's work shows us exactly where Hegelian speculation and scientific biblical scholarship takes us, as well as pointing out useful features of the utter poverty of the middle-class, burgher religion of his own Golden Age Denmark. Kierkegaard happily concurs with Feuerbach about the natural human tendency to construct religion as the ultimate idol. To Kierkegaard—in keeping with Reformed Christianity's general suspicion of religion—this deep tendency towards religious idolatry is not the essence of Christianity, it is rather the essence of human sinfulness as expressed religiously. Kierkegaard is also appreciative

3. See, for example, Marx, "A Contribution to the Critique of Hegel's Philosophy of Right" in Tucker, *The Marx-Engels Reader*, 55.

of Feuerbach's candor. For if one wishes to reason from purely scientific and rational premises in the Hegelian dialectical manner, then the only reasonable place to land is self-worshipping atheism. (Though, agreeing with Hamann, Kierkegaard does not think such scientific and rational purity possible and he considers Hegelianism to be pretentious abstract speculation.) To Kierkegaard, Feuerbach does the Christian world the great service of making it crystal clear how preposterous it is to attempt to be a Christian and also pursue scientistic biblicism and Hegelian speculative philosophy.[4]

Both Marx and Kierkegaard had a strong appreciation for the work of Feuerbach, while both, in different ways, were critical of Feuerbach's Hegelianism. Yet while they read the final significance of *The Essence of Christianity* in opposite directions, it is important to see what Kierkegaard and Marx had in common, as well as what they had in difference.

In common, both Marx and Kierkegaard are interested in the way in which religious beliefs shape the actual practice of day-to-day life, and of that life as lived in relation to others and the material conditions of life. In this regard, Kierkegaard is as recognizably sociological as Marx. However, what completely separates Kierkegaard from Marx is Kierkegaard's refusal to swing to a functionally materialist first philosophy as the interpretive ground from which the real meaning of religion and social relations can be discerned. This separates Kierkegaard not only from Marx, but from the mainstream of the social science trajectory that was to follow on from Marx and other powerful progressive thinkers in the nineteenth century.

WORSHIP AND SOCIOLOGY: RUNNING THE 1840S AGAIN, BUT DIFFERENTLY

Looking back at the 1840s from the present, what we can see is the possibility of a theologically grounded sociology in Kierkegaard's

4. Kierkegaard, *Philosophical Fragments*, 217–18. See also Malesic, "Illusion and Offense in *Philosophical Fragments*: Kierkegaard's Inversion of Feuerbach's Critique of Christianity."

work. Back then, theologically premised sociology *could* have taken off, because the functional paradigms and seminal works of what we now call the social and human sciences were not yet locked down. But, apart from Kierkegaard, that opportunity was not taken up at the time.

In this little book, my first task is to describe what Kierkegaard's theological sociology looked like. I am not doing this just to show an interesting historical pathway that was signaled but not taken back in the 1840s. I am writing this book because I think Kierkegaard was on the right track then, and that in many regards our prevailing functionally materialist social sciences—which have largely followed Marx's lead—provide us with an interpretive framework that is simply wrong.

I am not writing this book as an anti-Marxist or as an enemy of the social sciences. Rather, I hold that the knowledge of society we now have is fascinating, but its interpretation within academia is—ironically—highly useful for the perpetuation of an anthropocentric form of religion, which Justin Welby calls Mammon.[5] So with the 1840s, I think that religion provides us with the deepest categories of understanding socio-economic power structures, but with Kierkegaard, I think only a genuinely *theological* interpretation of religion provides us with an adequate interpretation of the meaning of social power structures.[6] To Kierkegaard, worship—as both an inescapable feature of individual human existence, and as an inescapable feature of collective and public life—and the reality of God are fundamental to any valid sociological knowledge.

Let us go back to the 1840s then to find fresh ways forward now. I think the time is now right to take up Kierkegaard's

---

5. See Welby, *Dethroning Mammon.*

6. It has to be pointed out that the great atheist thinkers of idolatry in the nineteenth century—Marx and Nietzsche—falsely appropriate the theological category of idolatry. In this regard they are theological charlatans. That is, they seek to disabuse one and all of any belief that human objects of worth and value can be anything other than idols, but then the point of their critique is not to promote the true worship of God, but rather to embrace the true worship of idols. Somehow we must create idols worthy of worship that we know we have fashioned ourselves, and in our own image.

theologically framed sociology and to go down the historical road not travelled back then.

2

Introducing Kierkegaard's Theological Sociology

KIERKEGAARD'S SOCIOLOGY IS GROUNDED in theology. This is not surprising, as *everything* Kierkegaard writes is grounded in theology. Indeed, in the 1840s it was not at all problematic to do sociology from theological premises because there was no sociological discipline as such. Any sort of theologically grounded sociology is a bit hard for us to imagine for we now typically assume that the methodological atheism of the established mainstream social sciences is obviously valid. Indeed, it was in the 1840s that not only a reductive positivism, but an explicit atheism, becomes the methodological premise of the new and progressive social sciences. So after the 1840s Kierkegaard's theological sociology looks, to us, seriously outdated. Or at least out of fashion. But . . . like Johann Georg Hamann, Kierkegaard has persuasive counter-Enlightenment *reasons* for bucking the dominant respectable intellectual trends of his times.[1]

More precisely, Kierkegaard was entirely happy for reductive positivists to be atheists, for scientistic historicists to disbelieve in miracles, for Kantian moralists to replace faith with rational moral

---

1. On H. G. Hamann, see Betz, *After Enlightenment*.

duty, and for speculative idealists to abandon orthodox Christian doctrine. What he found unacceptable was for Christian church-men and theologians to do the same. Kierkegaard refused to mildly go along with the prevailing intellectual trends of his times, not only because he was (becoming) a Christian and found those trends anathema to his commitments, piety, and practice of life, but because he had no confidence that those trends had any real validity, even in their own terms. Indeed, the perennial difficul-ties of rationalism and empiricism, their Kantian merger and their idealist transcendence, were clearly understood by Kierkegaard; his counter-Enlightenment disposition was not then—and not now—intellectually facile.

But Kierkegaard was bucking the trends, not only of what we might now call the secular academy, but of his church as well. By the early 1850s Kierkegaard thought that respectable Christian re-ligion and theology in his milieu was almost entirely functionally atheistic, and that it was almost impossible to be a professional cleric and also be a Christian.[2] It was not news to Kierkegaard that in his lifetime European intellectual life had lost the ability to sus-tain any sort of theological vision that would define, interpret, and inform any sort of existentially true knowledge.

I stress that Kierkegaard has *reasons* to oppose the nascent social scientific trends of his times, for Kierkegaard's thought in areas such as sociology is still often neglected on the grounds that, as an existential theologian, the secular and social aspects of his thought can be passed over as the work of an anti-rational indi-vidualist with a perverse taste for blindly leaping faith. This will not do.[3] Certainly Kierkegaard spurns the rationalism, positivism, and speculative idealism of his times, but this does not make him an irrational fideist. Further, his distinctly theological approach to what we would now call psychology and sociology is stunningly insightful, and it may well be that his analysis is so deep precisely

2. See Kierkegaard, *Attack Upon "Christendom."*

3. See Westphal, *Kierkegaard's Critique of Reason and Society.* From different angles see also Phillips, *Faith and Philosophical Enquiry* and Evans, *Passionate Reason.*

because it does *not* assume methodological atheism and because it is embedded in an explicitly theological anthropology.

The most sustained treatment Kierkegaard gives to theological sociology is *Two Ages*. This is an astonishing little text, and well worth exploring.

THE *TWO AGES*

In 1846 Kierkegaard published what he creatively described as a literary review of a novel by his fellow Dane, Thomasine Gyllembourg. This novel depicts the interactions between two generations in the same household in order to highlight how very different the *Zeitgeists* are that shaped the life histories and outlooks of each generation. The operational assumptions and life objectives of these uncomfortably cohabiting generations are defined by radically different epochal landscapes. Hence the title of Gyllembourg's novel is *Two Ages*.

The older generation in this story knows the passionate glory, the world-changing turbulence, and the catastrophic destruction of the Napoleonic era. This generation had glorious and revolutionary ideals and the courage to enact them. They made bold and impassioned choices guided by their ideals, giving no thought to the upheaval or practical impossibilities of the lives they chose. These are the children of the Age of Revolution. The younger generation in Gyllembourg's novel is modelled after the norms of the comfortable burgher class in Golden Age Denmark. This is a calculating, stability-conscious generation, cool rather than passionate, self-concerned and inherently suspicious of impractical and costly grand ideals. These are the children of the Present Age. Gyllembourg makes no judgment as to which age is better, but allows the reader to see how the characters shaped by both ages act in a manner that is understandable in the light of the formative influences of the age to which they belong.

Kierkegaard's book-length "literary review" draws extensively on Gyllembourg's masterful novel, but he has little critical interest in the form and effectiveness of the writing or of the technical skill of the writer. Rather, because this novel evokes and clarifies many thoughts that Kierkegaard has about revolution and the spirit of the Golden Age of Denmark, the novel becomes an opportunity for him to present to us his own thoughts as facilitated by the poignant narrative of the novel.

The third section of Kierkegaard's *Two Ages* is where Kierkegaard uses Gyllembourg's categories of the Age of Revolution and the Present Age for his own sociological explorations.[4] Here we find Kierkegaard's most sustained account of how—amongst other things—the public and the press work in an age that is *not* defined by passionate believers in high ideas. This text clearly locates Kierkegaard as a thinker who was profoundly engaged with the public world in which he lived, and who was keenly aware of the larger political events of Europe in the 1840s.

What is most striking here is that what Kierkegaard describes and critiques as the Present Age of his time—an age characterized by a spiritually superficial public and by a banal and manipulative press—was only then in its embryonic form, but the essential characteristics of that age have greatly matured in our times. The forward-looking accuracy of his analysis is remarkable.

In terms outlined by Abraham Heschel, Kierkegaard sociological analysis stands in the prophetic tradition.[5] The prophet is someone who sees to the heart of what is going on in any given community, and sees where it is going, because s/he is attuned to that which is most basic for any people; the health or sickness of the relation of a people to God. At this point—given the great success of non-theologically defined sociocultural analysis in the academy since the 1840s—we need to introduce thought categories that have been excluded from the social science if we are to grasp Kierkegaard's insights. In particular, we need to understand what worship means as a sociocultural category.

---

4. Kierkegaard, *Two Ages*, 60–112. Hereafter this text will be referred to as *TA* in the notes.

5. See Heschel, *The Prophets*. See also Walter Brueggemann, *The Prophetic Imagination*.

THE DOXOLOGICAL DIAGNOSTIC FRAMEWORK
OF THE PRESENT AGE

Kierkegaard's sociology is doxological.

We are familiar with "a doxology" as a noun, (a song of praise or blessing in a religious service) but this does not help us in understanding "the doxological" more broadly as an adjective, and—in the way I am using it—it does not help us understand "doxology" as an evaluative framework.

Doxa, as the term has evolved within Judeo-Christian usage, means the manifest glory of God. *Doxa* in classical Greek means opinion, appearance, and common belief, but when the Septuagint translated *kavod* (the manifest glory of God) as *doxa*, this word became deeply associated with worship in Greco-Roman Judaism. Apprehending and acknowledging the glory of God is now deeply associated with *doxa*, as worship. For the most basic responsive currency of worship—the affirmation of true and ultimate worth—is the praise of God. There are other currencies as well; notably, one third of the Psalms are songs of lament, this is the shadow-side of the manifest presence of God—complaint about the apparent absence of divine presence, the distressing absence of protection and vindication for the true worshipper in the experience of injustice, slander, oppression, etc. But all prayer, all theology, all religious liturgy, every act and essence of our being as worshiping animals, should arise out of an appreciation of the goodness, the majesty, the glory of God.

Thinking anthropologically within a Judeo-Christian theological framework, worship is central to the partial attainment (or the tragic loss) of that quality of existence the Hebrew scriptures call "life" (Deut 30:19–20). The first four of the Ten Commandments pertain to right worship; the last six to moral injunctions (Deut 5:6–21). Have no other god before the LORD your God is the first commandment, and, as affirmed in the Shema Yisrael (Deut 6:4–9; 11:13–21; Num 15:37–41), it is the right ordering of love that makes the peace, blessing, and life of God accessible to the people. This outlook is stated in the Christian scriptures as well

(Mark 12:29–31). If one loves God first, if the first and final object of ultimate worth (*worth*-ship) orienting the values, meanings, and loyalties in the practice, habits, relationships, and ambitions of one's life is the one true God, then the life of the worshipper (and the worshipping community) is rightly ordered. Then the life of God is given to God's covenant people, and the dwelling of God's glory will rest among those people. So to worship God alone is to place the center of value and meaning in the God who made us, rather than in an object of worth of our own making—an idol—or in activities defined by our own physical needs (hence the significance of the Sabbath to the Hebrews). This point needs to be labored here because Kierkegaard simply assumes a doxological outlook, though we, now living in a global knowledge and power culture shaped by a predominantly post-Christian West, do not well understand the concept of worship or idols any more.

But here is the rub: if one does not take worship into account as the defining signature of what it means to be human—in *all* contexts of our life—one is not thinking *as a Christian* about what it means to be human. The idea that worship is a discretely religious activity, performed only in discretely religious times and places, and defined by distinctive emotional states and rituals, fails to understand a Christian anthropology entirely.[6] We are particularly prone to this misunderstanding because the secular life-world we live in assumes that worship is an optional private religious freedom that people have that is separated out from the public and practical arenas of life. Our very way of life assumes that worship is located only in the inner world of personal belief convictions. But Kierkegaard does not believe this for a moment. Whilst religion

6. I do not mean to denigrate religious ritual here. The initiation of the sacrament of marriage, for instance, should be performed in a solemn yet joyful religious and ritual manner, orienting conjugal love and family life to its highest sacramental meaning in the love of Christ for the church, and pledging the governing of familial love by the Christian love of God and neighbor. But then that religious ritual of the wedding is not discrete from the life of the married couple. The religious ritual needs to be lived out in the meaning of that ritual for as long as the married couple shall both live. Religion that has any depth of meaning cannot be privately discrete from the non-religious, or from ordinary social relations and all the mundane activities of daily life.

can—and should—play a positive formational and performative role in our worship (though it can certainly be a hindrance to worship and a site of idolatry) the idea that worship *could* be reduced to a discretely religious category is hopelessly existentially unrealistic to Kierkegaard. The orientation of the soul to God—in both love and fear, faith and sin, truth and lies—is what defines our actual human existence. Any attempt to understand social norms and structures without tying these things back to worship is itself a fantastic abstraction. Unsurprisingly, Kierkegaard looks at how society works, and he is able to judge whether it is working in a way that promotes or hinders human flourishing, through the lens of worship.

KIERKEGAARD'S DOXOLOGICAL KEY

The core doxological idea of Kierkegaard's critique of the Present Age is remarkably simple.

> The idolized positive principle of sociality in our age is the consuming, demoralizing principle that in the thralldom of reflection transforms even virtues into *vitia splendida* [glittering vices].[7] And what is the basis of this other than a disregard for the separation of the religious individual before God in the responsibility of eternity.[8]

To Kierkegaard, everything else in life is a derivative function of the sickness or health of the relation of each individual to their first object of worship. Thus, doxology is the ground of the principle of sociality that shapes our moral norms and that governs the desires, purposes, and the very identities of individuals within our shared way of life. Putting worship, putting the sickness or health of the relation of the individual to a frame of ultimate and

---

7. This is a Latin reference to a phrase by Tertullian. Tertullian's idea that the virtues of pagan Rome are actually vices due to their doxological failure, is expounded in Augustine's *City of God*, XIX, 25.

8. *TA*, 86.

transcendent meaning, as the bedrock of the principle of sociality is the core interpretive feature of Kierkegaard's sociology.

As already mentioned, when Kierkegaard wrote *Two Ages*, a doxologically framed conception of human sociality was not a radical idea. Indeed, the idea that religion could be understood without any reference to the reality of God was the radical new idea that was causing such ferment in Germany and beyond. The 1840s was a key juncture in the shift of the progressive Western intelligentsia towards what Charles Taylor calls the immanent frame.[9] But this side of that juncture it is easy for us to notice how perceptive Kierkegaard was about the mass media age that was to come, without paying much attention to why he was so perceptive. But the "why" is crucial. Kierkegaard reads our age like an open book because he is not assuming an immanent frame of sociological meaning. More precisely, Kierkegaard is noticing that "a disregard for the separation of the religious individual before God in the responsibility of eternity"[10] is the governing functional feature of his age, and he looks at that feature as its core pathology.

That is, any individual who does not willingly repose in the most primary relation of human existence—the relation of the soul to God—will look in vain for themselves in the exterior reflections of personal and community identity afforded to them by every secondary relation. This idolatrous looking in vain drives the social and psychological dynamics of the Present Age. Because of a primary existential lack, the secondary—though good as secondary—becomes an idol, and an idol that cannot grant the individual a meaningful, spiritually substantive self. For this reason the Present Age is paralyzed in relation to passionate action, is—ironically—essentially preoccupied with trivialities, superficialities, and illusions, and is profoundly blind to all matters of genuine importance. Thus, in the Present Age both the public and its press illustrate the banality of the illusional reflected sociality that is appropriate to the inner spiritual emptiness of the people of its age.

[margin note: this idolatry as societal pathology.]

9. See Taylor, *A Secular Age*.
10. *TA*, 86.

The soul's relation to God is the most primary feature of human identity to Kierkegaard. This is unremarkably orthodox within Christian theology. But what is remarkable is that both psychology and sociology have defined themselves as sciences in ways that have decisively delineated themselves from Christian theology since Kierkegaard's time. In fact, the central moves in this delineation, this exclusion of theology from psychology, anthropology, and sociology, were going on in the 1830s and 40s. As a result of German liberal Protestant innovations, a modern historical science of biblical interpretation was constructed from the turn of the nineteenth century, producing David Strauss' naturalistic reconstruction of the life of Jesus where the scientifically incredible (i.e., the creedal orthodox) features of the Christian religion were understood as non-factual mythologies. Once theologians treated the incarnation and the resurrection of Christ as non-factual myths, this gave non-theologians license to entirely re-think the nature and meaning of religion in non-theological terms. So, hot on the heels of David Strauss comes the naturalistic anthropological interpretation of religion by Ludwig Feuerbach. This in turn is followed rapidly by the materialist sociology of Karl Marx. Freudian psychology would eventually arise from that German trajectory, which would then be followed by behaviorist and other materialist conceptions of the soul and the nature of society.

What Kierkegaard's core analytic idea from *Two Ages* points out is that no science of society is independent of its conception of the human soul—its psychology. Every sociology is embedded in a philosophical anthropology that shapes the way we understand what any person essentially is, and what persons-in-relations actually are. Starting a sociology from a materialist anthropology is going to make it entirely impossible to see what Kierkegaard sees about how society functions. But if it is actually true that the soul is an inherently theologically situated entity, then Kierkegaard's sociology is going to be strikingly more realistic than any understanding of society embedded in the assumptions of materialist positivity.

Let us now take an overview of how society within the Present Age looks to Kierkegaard.

KEY MOTIFS IN THE PRESENT AGE:

The Revolutionary, as High Idolatry

Kierkegaard muses that the passionate age of Napoleon had rational form and a spiritually dynamic culture that arose naturally from the inward vitality of its individuals.[11] Significantly, however, Kierkegaard does not idealize that revolutionary age, for it is no less idolatrous than the spiritually insipid age to which he compares it.[12] Indeed, the Age of Revolution has a higher idolatry than the Present Age. The Age of Revolution is a secularized but deeply religious age, where the individual chooses an immediate and passionate commitment to the absolute, which gives ideology the characteristic of revelation and the political ideal something approaching the glory of God. These false ultimates and misplaced primary passions cannot finally spiritually carry the individual or create the eschaton, but they are touched with a genuine glory because "the highest idea . . . is the religious."[13] That is, there is a spiritual wellspring in high idolatry that is modelled after the religious, and this is culturally superior to the Present Age where our idolatry is constructed out of mere mundane egoism. For the mundane ego is an object of worship that provides no transcendent pole star to give the soul its primary identity and that gives the soul no object of passion that is religiously worthy of a soul. Thus, the age characterized by low idolatry has far less spiritual vitality than the age characterized by high idolatry.

Yet, whether the mundane material self of the Present Age or the high political idea of the Age of Revolution is the primary

11. *TA*, 61–62.

12. *TA*, 65–66.

13. *TA*, 65.

object of worth, both are idols. For, as Kierkegaard's core idea implies, when the soul orients itself in a primary manner to anything other than God, this doxological failure produces pathologies of one type or another. As Kierkegaard sees it, the soul, as a creature and not as its own creator, is unable to establish its identity in any true and primary way outside of its relation to God.

Even so, there are grades of quality in idolatry. Doxologically, ecclesiologically, and eschatologically, revolutionaries are much admired by Kierkegaard. Ideally, each revolutionary individual has something approaching an inner solidity that is expressed through their decisive actions because they seek to passionately live an eschatologically transformative idea. The kind of unity in passionate action that true revolutionaries have is grounded in each revolutionary's particular inward relation of ultimate commitment to the same idea. This is, actually, more like what the church in theological reality is than is often manifest in the church. In this manner, revolutionaries shame the small-minded, self-concerned, comfortable-church respectability of the Present Age. When, in his final years, Kierkegaard rails against respectable Danish Lutheranism, it is clear that in his vision of godless revolutionaries, as painted by Gyllembourg, they understand the type of commitments and fellowship he expects from the church far better than do his fellow Christians.

Because the revolutionary has a form of doxological commitment to something genuinely above the self, a doxology that is worthy of a soul, this dynamic produces a very different kind of collective action to the conformist herd mentality that Kierkegaard sees as characteristic of an age that has no high ideas and no passion to enact high ideals. The fact that each revolutionary is individually committed to something bigger than their own self-interest, something that transcends their self, gives, paradoxically, that self its substantiality and makes true community between differentiated and concretely particular substantive selves possible.[14] Yet,

> [r]emove the relation to oneself and we have the tumultuous self-relating of the mass to an idea; but remove this as well, and we have crudeness.[15]

Three Life-Forms: High Revolutionary Idolatry, Mass Ideology Idolatry, Crudeness

In the above quote Kierkegaard marks three cultural life-forms. Firstly, there is the cultural life-form characterized by the fellowship of impassioned individuals who are united in their distinct and inner relation to the same ideal. Secondly, there is the cultural life-form that results from the degeneration of the revolutionary life-form into a mass relation to an idea. Here the concrete particularity and personal responsibility of the individual is lost and the ideal grows into a strange and tyrannical abstraction as if it were a thing in itself, rather than a thing that responsible and passionate individuals believe, will, and enact. This is the dynamic unleashing the reign of terror in the French Revolution; the integrity of the individual is entirely lost here. Thirdly, there is the cultural life-form that results from the degeneration of a tyrannical mass ideology into an atomized post-ideological herd society. Here safety is secured, but there are neither substantial individuals nor an ecclesia of people united in any high reality; it is all crudeness in the end. Kierkegaard calls the era in which this third life-form is dominant, the Present Age.

14. *TA*, 62: "The person who is essentially turned inward because he is essentially impassioned for an idea is never crude. . . . [Thus] when individuals (each one individually) are essentially and passionately related to an idea and together are essentially related to the same idea, the relation is optimal and normative. Individually the relation separates them (each one has himself for himself), and ideally it unites them."

15. *TA*, 63.

23

The Present Age

Once this third life-form has become established, the loss of faith in ideas and in anything that transcends the individual results in a life-form of narrow and pragmatic egotism. Here

> people shove and . . . rub against each other in point-
> less externality. . . . [Here] individuals do not in inward-
> ness turn away from each other, do not turn outwards
> in unanimity for an idea, but naturally turn to each
> other in a frustrating and suspicious, aggressive, level-
> ling reciprocity.[16]

A key feature of this third life-form—the life-form Kierkeg-
aard calls the Present Age—is **levelling**. No one must stand out, everyone must conform; and yet this is also an excessively suspi-
cious and competitive life-form. Here winners are those who do what everyone else does and want what everyone else wants—they have no individuality—but they do it at the expense of others and as measured against their relative standing amongst those who have essentially the same quantifiable desires. They have no inner life to speak of which is not contingently defined by externally normative behaviors, opinions, acquisitions, and relations.

Another key feature of the absence of high ideas in the Present Age is **talkativeness**. Talkativeness is a parody of real commu-
nication because where an age is no longer defined by individuals who cleave passionately and actively to a meaning higher than themselves, higher than their externally defined needs, then there is nothing meaningful to say. There is also nothing essentially meaningful to do. With astonishing prescience Kierkegaard as seer surveys the age of jet travel, the internet, and contemporary financial markets and incisively prefigured Jacques Ellul's critique of the technological society.

> [Those of the Present Age] shut themselves out from . . .
> the rebirth of passion by talkativeness. Suppose that such
> an age has invented the swiftest means of transportation
> and communication, has unlimited combined financial

16. *TA*, 63.

resources: how ironic that the velocity of the transportation system and the speed of communication stand in an inverse relationship to the dilatoriness of irresolution.[17]

Ellul notes that the driving principle of our technological society is efficiency, to the exclusion of teleology, and to the negation of any metaphysically or religiously framed notion of ultimacy.[18] Thus, the capacity merely to *do* things, and to do them always faster, better, cheaper, but without any high or intrinsic reason *to* do things, characterizes the frenetic activism of the options-open instrumental potency of our age. Thus, under a *Zeitgeist* without a passionate religious horizon Kierkegaard proposes an inverse relationship between technological advances in transportation, communication, and action, and any good reason to go anywhere, the capacity to communicate anything worth saying, and the will to do anything decisively valuable. Thus, **gossip**, **entertainment**, and **chatter** come to dominate the forums of both public and private discourse.[19] These distracting, filling, and petty cultural signatures arise because the failure of individual inwardness in the Present Age means there is nothing of transcendent seriousness or inherent meaningfulness that is passionately believed in the life-form norms that define the age.

Naturally enough, when there are no big ideas, no high "beyond" that relativizes the contingency and transience in which the self is situated, the spiritual vitality of a culture is drained. Where there is nothing ultimate beyond the self to give human culture and enterprise its spiritual dimension, the Present Age—for all its instrumental power and technological cleverness—is characterized by the absence of grandeur; by **littleness**.

> As soon as the individual no longer has essential enthusiasm . . . his life becomes garrulous, . . . the whole thing becomes a flux, a blend of a little resolution and a little situation, a little prudence and a little courage, a

17. *TA*, 63–64.
18. See Ellul, *The Technological Society*.
19. *TA*: gossip, 78; entertainment, 94; chatter 97.

little probability and a little faith, a little action and a little incident.[20]

Without a religious horizon of some form—be it an atheistic revolutionary ideology or whatever—only the practical and only the sensual gains purchase on the values, rationality, and goals of the age. Thus:

> [t]he present age is essentially a sensible, reflecting age, devoid of passion, flaring up in superficial, short-lived enthusiasm and prudentially relaxing in indolence.[21]

Reflection—Glittering Mirrors for the Empty Self

Kierkegaard is sociologically fascinated by the outlook he calls reflection. This is the Present Age's propensity to very carefully examine, judge, know about, and master everything. Yet all the judgments and knowledge of this reflection are measured in terms of externalities and practicalities without any vital inner sense of value or ultimate purpose. Thus the double meaning of reflection here is that this age is very thoughtful, but it is only thoughtful about the *surface reflections* of things—inner meanings, higher purposes, and intrinsically valuable ends are entirely opaque to the Present Age. There can be no *summum bonum*, no highest good, in such an age. There is only the glittering externality of surfaces. These reflecting exterior surfaces are mirrors, and are used in the Present Age as a means of trying to find the missing self. Constructing external images of ourselves, for ourselves, and as a means of commodifying the self and others, is a key feature of the Present Age.

It is disturbing to read Kierkegaard's *Two Ages*—written in the 1840s—and to notice how astutely his observations reach into our Present Age. He sees into our age where publicity has become more important than reality and where the individual is drowned

20. *TA*, 67.

21. *TA*, 68. Note; this definition of the Present Age is entirely italicized in the original.

in a relentless flood of miscellaneous announcements;[22] he sees into our age of politics, which has no high ideals and where our leaders are merely reactive within what is accepted by all as externally necessary realism;[23] he sees an age governed by excessive externally referenced procedures, though without any notion of the requirements of substantive moral principles;[24] he sees culture where immodesty, impropriety, and philandering are normative;[25] he sees the rise of self-infatuated identity publicity such as is all too easy to find on Facebook and other social media platforms[26]— there is not much about the inner workings of our times he has not noticed from afar. And he sees the rise of public opinion and the central role the mass media plays in feeding the need of the public of the Present Age for a specific kind of opinion—the factual, realist, useful, and manipulative *public* opinion that we now call the news, information, and advertising, and which Jacques Ellul calls *propagandes.*[27]

We will continue unpacking Kierkegaard's ideas about the Present Age as we go, but his outlook on the press is particularly interesting and opens up the big question of causality in socio-cultural dynamics.

THE PUBLIC, THE PRESS, AND CAUSALITY IN SOCIO-CULTURAL DYNAMICS

Kierkegaard maintains that in the Present Age the public is a levelling abstraction and the press is its dog.[28] That is—bearing in mind Kierkegaard's core diagnostic idea—the press in the Present Age is a function of the public of the Present Age, which is in turn a

22. *TA*, 70.

23. *TA*, 107.

24. *TA*, 100–102.

25. *TA*, 64, 101–3.

26. *TA*, 102: "The exhibitionist tendency is the self-infatuation of the conceit of reflection."

27. See Ellul, *Propaganda.*

28. *TA*, 93–96.

function of the spiritual poverty of the individuals of the Present Age, and not the other way around. In other words, Kierkegaard's outlook maintains that failure in the relation of the "religious individual before God in the responsibility of eternity"[29] causes the public of the Present Age to arise, which in turn requires a distinctive type of press that will loyally serve the spiritual poverty of that public.

The above notion of causality strikes the empirical, statistical, structurally mechanistic, and progressive economico-political sensibilities of the social scientific outlook on culture as laughably heterodox. Typically, the social sciences assume that large-scale socio-economic forces govern culture and are thus the primary drivers that causally shape the formation of individual norms, beliefs, and behaviors. But while Kierkegaard certainly sees the relationship between the press and the public as dialectic, he sees that relationship itself as a function of a religious dynamic that is not primarily grounded in the economic interest of the prevailing status quo, but in the relation of the individual to the religious.[30] The Present Age fosters a widespread illness in this primary

29. *TA*, 86.

30. There is undoubtedly a profoundly unequal power relationship between large social, cultural, and economic forces and the individual. Max Horkheimer and Theodor Adorno accurately note that "the basis on which technology acquires power over society is the power of those whose economic hold over society is greatest" (*Dialectic of Enlightenment*, 121). Macro-cultural powers do indeed have a highly psychologically and sociologically intelligent vested interest in forever priming, defining, and driving the desires of the atomized individual towards gratification via the consumption, entertainment, and fantasy opportunities consumer society provides. This needs to be recognized and the sedating and manipulating agenda of this reality needs to be named and structurally resisted. Marxist analysis can be very helpful to those ends. A Kierkegaardian perspective in no manner denies the force of the macro-cultural powers at work within the Present Age. However, the Kierkegaardian perspective places the micro-cultural—the relation of the individual to culture—as ontologically prior to the macro-cultural because the religious situation of the individual is seen as ontologically and concretely prior to the powerful collective abstractions of dominant trends in both culture and politico-economic structures and nodes of interest. This is why one individual of sufficient religious inwardness—Gandhi, for example—can have a real effect on culture and power.

relationship, which gives rise to a spiritually levelling public under post-revolutionary conditions. Thus, it is *this* religiously dysfunctional public that feeds its press and keeps it alive, and the press plays to the affections and interests of *this* public, as well as attacking those who are seen as a threat by *this* public.

To Kierkegaard the public of the Present Age names a demonic abstract power that is bigger than the sum of the particular actions of the concrete individuals who comprise it.[31] The demonic here is not the cause of individual choices, but is thrown up by individual choices that are idolatrously orientated. Further, as the underlying spirit of the age behind both the public and the press actively affirms the absence of inner spiritual distinctiveness in the individuals who comprise that age, anyone who in some way stands out from the norm of inner indistinctiveness must be levelled by the public. All who have what Kierkegaard calls inwardness or essential passion, all who have some form of primitive contact with primary meaning, all who have tasted some measure of the spiritual water that arises from the soul's inner well, all who seek to live within the "how" of a soul related to an ultimate truth that transcends the tiny competitive world of the atomized individual, are outsiders to the Present Age. As such they are a threat to the uniformly unremarkable inner norms and the externalized and instrumental values affirmed by the public. Fortunately for the Present Age, many people with inner religious substance can be ignored due to the irrelevance of inner life to the public realm under the conditions of the Present Age. But if for some reason the spiritually alive are not ignored, they must be handed over to the dog of the public (the press) for a good mauling. They can be made into the object of celebrity entertainment, they can be vilified as fanatical extremists, or they can be simply lampooned and ridiculed by handing them over to the herd mentality of the press for jeering and trampling, simply because they are not running with the herd.

In sum, Kierkegaard sees the socio-cultural and political dynamics of the Present Age as arising from an absence of individual inner religious responsibility, an absence that Kierkegaard

31. *TA*, 86.

finds most horrifyingly at home in the very heart of Danish state endorsed Lutheranism.[32] Kierkegaard sees religious and existential concerns as driving social, cultural, and political trends. The manner in which the press serves to aid and defend a spiritually vacuous public is seen by Kierkegaard to illustrate this dynamic aptly. But can Kierkegaard's outlook be taken seriously? Has history left the possibility of a theological sociology behind?

We will now look a little more closely at the way in which non-theologically defined social scientific thought developed in the 1840s and the latter half of the twentieth century before looking at whether Kierkegaard's outlook should be treated as a historical curiosity, or an approach that remains viable to this day.

32. See Kierkegaard, *Attack on "Christendom"*; Kierkegaard, *Christian Discourses.*

3

Kierkegaard at the 1840s Fork

IN TERMS OF THE way the social sciences developed in the nineteenth century, Kierkegaard's sociology travels down the very short arm of a historical fork where the mainstream went the other way. The manner in which "the religious" was interpreted sociologically is the key distinguishing feature separating Kierkegaard from Marx, the first of the three classical sociologists, and this remains the central area of difference between the social sciences as established disciplines, largely formed by classical sociology, and Kierkegaard's work, to this day.[1]

1. See: van Krieken et al. *Sociology*, 22–29 for a fine introductory sociology textbook history of the development of modern sociology. The standard story starts with the rise of classical sociology via Comte, Marx, and Spencer as a response to the social and economic upheavals of the Industrial Revolution and the presumed collapse of religion as an intellectually viable means of interpreting and unifying the social world. At the turn of the twentieth century sociology continued on this trajectory and became an accepted academic discipline via Durkheim and Weber. The 1920s is when US sociology kicked in with a focus on urbanization opening the door to interpretive and symbolic readings of social meaning in anthropology and in the context of social change. The 1940s–60s saw the rise of functionalist sociology in Durkheim's shadow, followed by conflict theory in the 1970s, leading up to feminist influence in the 1980s. Things were moving away from the positivism of classical sociology as cultural meaning became understood to be inextricable from social function. By the late 1980s postmodern theorists and the social

The 1840s is probably the decade when what we now recognize as the social scientific outlook gained something of an irresistible leverage on the intellectual climate of European high culture. It is this outlook that effectively sidelined Kierkegaard's religiously embedded socio-cultural and psychological analysis of existence. Going back to the 1840s, then, gives us an opportunity to re-evaluate this significant transition to the modern scientific study of society, and the fact that Kierkegaard overtly and consciously did not make that transition helps us to see what issues are at stake in how we understand what is causal and what is real and what is secondary and what is illusory when we think about society and its workings.

Kierkegaard was keenly aware of the intellectual currents of his time that produced the social scientific outlook.[2] Mathematically reductive mechanistic determinism in the affairs of

---

and cultural upheavals of globalization had a strong influence on sociology. Where we now sit is that social and cultural constructivism, and the situation of social and cultural interpretation being located within the culture and structures it interprets, make any naïve conception of sociological facts impossible, and yet the discipline as a whole has its genesis in the rejection of religion as a viable means of understanding cultural and social meaning. So it is now possible to reason from any set of interpretive commitments—including religious ones—but all interpretive commitments are seen as constructed. While Kierkegaard's and Hamann's stance is deeply aware of the imaginative and situated human tissue of all human meaning, the two things that still separates them out from where sociological constructivism and the postmodern critique of positive has gone is Kierkegaard's and Hamann's understanding of divine revelation operating within, but not being reducible to, the context of social construction, and of the ontological foundation of the human condition transcending mere social construction and biological necessity.

2. This is clearly illustrated in *Philosophical Fragments*, wherein Kierkegaard critiques the modern philosophical methodology of doubt, as if faith was not necessary for any approach to truth, and in the *Concluding Unscientific Postscript to Philosophical Fragments,* were he critiques the modern tendency to grant truth to naturalistically understood de-mythologized historical facts. Also the influence of Johann Georg Hamann can be powerfully seen in Kierkegaard, where the revelation of God within history cannot be reduced to a rationally or scientifically decipherable facticity. See Betz, *After Enlightenment* for a magnificent outline of Hamann's astonishing alternative to the Kantian/ Hegelian trajectory taken by nineteenth-century Germanic philosophy.

human history and the human soul—the outlook of the modern social sciences and modern psychology—was a nascent possibility for the mainstream of Western intellectual culture from the time of Galileo.[3] Yet it is the eighteenth-century triumph of the modern scientific outlook over Aristotelian natural philosophy in the academy—after Newton's *Philosophiae Naturalis Principia Mathematica* from the late seventeenth century—that signals the decisive cultural shift in this direction. In the aftermath of this new and powerful scientific natural philosophy, Kant endeavors to build a philosophical system that preserves a realm of human freedom within an entirely mechanically determined natural universe via positing rational moral universals that the human soul could freely decide to uphold. Here freedom consists in the capacity of the moral individual to choose what is rationally necessary, rather than what is merely instinctually or socially necessary. But such an outlook seemed inadequate to Hegel, for freedom here is not positive enough and does not escape determinism enough to uphold the spiritual dignity of reasoning and creating humanity. Hegel, rebelling against the unthinking determinates of mechanical nature, wanted the type of freedom that could *create* moral goodness and where the rational necessities of nature itself were conditioned and re-fashioned by the spirit of humanity. Hegel generates an astonishing system of rational dialectics that raises Spirit above the necessities of nature via the astonishing power of thought as thought evolves within time and culture.

Hegel was the dominant figure of German philosophy when Kierkegaard was a young man at university, and little Denmark was typically in the intellectual shadow of her great German neighbor. But Kierkegaard, like other bright young radicals of his era, found Hegel's astonishing achievements in abstract thought as strangely missing the mark of actual existence. Hegel believed he had subsumed historical existence into the spiritual essence of pure thought, but this integration seemed like a merely conservative philosophical sleight of hand to the young radicals in Berlin

---

3. See Henry, *Barbarism*, 102–6 on the anti-existential tendencies of "Galilean science."

of the 1830s and 1840s. In 1841, ten years after Hegel's death, Kierkegaard attended the lectures of Schelling in Berlin where Schelling—to Kierkegaard's great excitement—spelled out why philosophically comprehended essence (*quid sit, what* it is) and actual existence (*quod sit, that* it is) cannot be conflated after the Hegelian manner. Here Kierkegaard realized that existence must be prior to thought or else thought is mere vacuous fantasy. Kierkegaard realized that—contra Hegel—one cannot rationally abstract oneself into eternity. The relation of the soul to God *within* existence alone gives access—and in a derived and secondary manner—to valid thought regarding essence. That is, the "how" of one's actual relation to God is prior to the "what" of philosophical or theological truth, and no amount of correct "what" knowledge can produce the correct "how" relation, which is alone decisive in existence.

Yet Kierkegaard's religiously grounded existentialism as a response to Hegel was not even considered by the atheist radicals who were to define the new direction in progressive social thought in the latter half of the nineteenth century. These thinkers happily accepted Hegel's positioning of thought concretely within the cultural evolution of human history, but they entirely occluded Hegel's notion of speculative essence—of Spirit. Existence as materially concerned practices embedded within history replaced speculative thought and Spirit entirely. This move—foundational to the modern social sciences—is premised on the assumption that the essence of humanity and society is in fact material; hence religion is in fact anthropology (the famous foundation of all Marxist critique) and there can be no "spiritual beyond" that is the soul of religion.

It is interesting to note not only how profoundly Kierkegaard differs from the materialistic young Hegelians, but how much he also has in common with them. Kierkegaard was highly critical of Hegel, and he was a direct contemporary of the Young Hegelians, who were also highly critical of Hegel. Indeed Kierkegaard read at least two of these young Hegelians—Strauss and Feuerbach—carefully.[4] Kierkegaard and these radicals were deeply interested in the nexus between religion and what we would now call cultural life-forms and economic and political practices.[5] Both Kierkegaard and the young Hegelians found the completion of religion in philosophy, which Hegel postulated, and Hegel's idealization of reason to the conservative neglect of action and existence, to be untenable.

In 1841, when Kierkegaard visited Berlin—the heartland of the young Hegelians and the intellectual center of German philosophy—he arrives at a critical juncture in what was the simultaneous birth of progressive radical atheism and the materialist social scientific methodology. On November 15, 1841, Karl Marx and Kierkegaard where both in the same crowded lecture theatre listening to Schelling's critique of Hegel.[6] Marx, the most famous of the young Hegelians, was to become the first of the three patriarchs of classical sociology and the impact of broadly progressive positivism in thinking about the nature of society and the psyche has dominated Western high culture since the mid-nineteenth century.

So in going to the 1840s we go back to a significant fork in the road in the critique of religion and the birth of the social sciences. At this point, the critique of religion and society could have gone down Kierkegaard's path—a critique that arises from within a profoundly theological stance—though it did not; or it could have gone down Marx's path—a critique that takes religion very seriously, but as an entirely humanly constructed phenomena. The

4. And, as Malantschuk carefully argues, Kierkegaard also unwittingly read Marx. We know Kierkegaard read a book published by Arnold Ruge in 1843 titled *Anekdota* in which there was a short article by Kein Berliner (a pseudonym under which Karl Marx wrote this article) titled *Luther als Schiedsrichter zwischen Strauss und Feuerbach* to which Kierkegaard refers. See Malantschuk, *The Controversial Kierkegaard*, 76–82.

5. On Kierkegaard's deep and persistent interest in the relationship between state-endorsed Lutheranism and the economic practices of the comfortable burgher class in Golden Age Denmark, see Pérez-Álvarez, *A Vexing Gadfly*.

6. Garff, *Søren Kierkegaard: A Biography*, 209.

later stance became dominant. This later stance either functionally or explicitly rejects the credibility of there being any knowable divine noumenon (reality) in which religious phenomena
(appearance) might partially participate. From Marx onward the
dominant streams in the social sciences would either assume materialist atheism, or apply a methodological atheism while seeking
to avoid all substantive theological claims.[7]

At this point I am going to stray forward just a little to the
1860s, to slightly nuance shades of conservative and progressive
thinking operating in the second half of the nineteenth century.
This sort of shading is important, for stark polarizations gain mo-
mentum in the twentieth rather than the nineteenth century. So,
very briefly, let us venture into the 1860s before coming back to the
1840s fork where Kierkegaard finds himself.

The end—and *not* the beginning—of the secularization of
the Western academy was largely achieved by the 1860s. This
secularization entailed the firm shifting of the divine to the realm
of subjective and unprovable conviction, delineating religious
belief from scientific knowledge. Finally, the long voyage towards
separating God from nature (and natural reality), which starts in
earnest with the sixteenth-century doctrine of *natura pura*, comes
in to port.[8] In the latter half of the nineteenth century, via a truth
conception defined by objective knowledge and a reductively
empirical conception of causation, a culturally viable functionally materialist realism becomes respectable. What was to become
social scientific thought in the twentieth century was largely at

7. John Milbank is right to point out that "Theology . . . purports to give
an ultimate narrative, to provide some ultimate depth of description. . . . Sur-
rendering this gaze to the various gazes of 'methodological atheism' would not
prove to be any temporary submission." Milbank, *Theology and Social Theory*,
253. This Kierkegaard also keenly saw in the 1840s.

8. On *natura pura* (pure nature) see Dupré, *Passage to Modernity*, 170–89,
206. *Natura pura* is the idea that nature does not need any ongoing divine
grace to be what it is. This is a doctrinal development that lead to thinking that
"nature" and the "supernatural" are fully separated and self-standing realms.
This is an astonishing departure from patristic and medieval doctrines of creation, where nature is embedded in the divine Logos for its intelligible forms,
and is continuously existentially dependent on God for its very being.

home with this way of thinking. But it must be remembered, it takes centuries of shifting ideas and life-world structures before this click into a new cultural cosmology, a new social metaphysics, can happen. The West in the nineteenth century, and even today, is deeply embedded in a culturally assumed conception of a divine source to reality, a divine logic expressed through nature, the divine gifting of meaning, value, essence, being, and purpose to the created cosmos, and of humanity as made in the image of God. But there is a point in time when this click to a culturally viable functional materialism happens. It arrives when Charles Darwin's *Origin of Species* hit the press in 1859. What Darwin's work offers us at this time is the possibility of a credible secular cosmogony that can locate our place within reality either with or without the God of traditional Western Christendom, or any God at all. Which is to say, when God is optional in thinking about our origins and essence, then God is functionally superfluous to our public life-form and its knowledge-structures. This is a very interesting moment. Even so, as with most cultural upheavals, this transition was not keenly felt by most in the late nineteenth century.

Looking back we can see this click point, but at the time it was by no means so obvious. Thinking of the second half of the nineteenth century, this was an era when conservatives in the academy and in influential institutions still assumed an integrated conception of divinity and nature. Yet these conservatives were in the same intellectual cooking pot as progressives who had either functionally separated divinity from nature or who had rejected the validity of the concept of the divine altogether. So, in very sweeping terms, there are roughly four parties, though Kierkegaard—at the preemptive historical juncture before the 1860s—fits none of them.

In the 1860s there were Conservative 1 (C1) types, who largely ignored the new social knowledge as it was obviously in some tension with the type of doctrinally traditional Creator-creation integrated outlook. Kierkegaard would have been sympathetic to this outlook as he thinks it a category error to pin questions of existential truth on the provisional and humanly constructed categories of the prevailing fashions in scientific knowledge and historical interpretation. Even so, Kierkegaard is anything but disinterested in what we would now call sociology and psychology, so he is not a C1. An anticlerical reading of Darwin, such as advanced by T. H. Huxley, tended to link the new biological naturalism in with progressive social reform agendas already linked to the new social sciences, and this kept C1 types largely interested in other things than social science and the origin of species.

Conservative 2 (C2) types were interested in the new sciences, and saw sometimes naïve, sometimes sophisticated ways of embracing a strictly methodologically materialist conception of objective knowledge while adapting rather than abandoning their conception of how the divine related to nature. Liberal Anglicanism was the fount of a great deal of natural science in England in the nineteenth century, and there was a tacit theological interest in applying the scientific method to biology and natural history. Liberal Anglican naturalists were comfortable constructing complex integrations of the new science with often deistic theology that was increasingly disconnected from creedal orthodoxy and supernaturalist thinking about the credibility of miracles and such. Why should not God be continuously creating by the process of competition and extinction? Why should we treat a pre-scientific mythic text (the Bible) as being in conflict with a very different type of knowledge discourse—science? This is an integrative stance that still somewhat privileges theological concerns in the manner in which the natural sciences are interpreted. It is not—at base—substantively committed to materialism, even if it is methodologically comfortable with a materialist outlook on positivity. Kierkegaard does not take this line as he is strongly familiar with what happens when you allow prevailing philosophical fashions (in his case, Danish Hegelianism) and what he saw as functionally atheist premises (as underpinning historical critical biblical exegesis) to set the terms of your own existential relation to God, the church, and the world.

Progressive 1 (P1) types functionally separated the subjective beliefs about the divine from factual knowledge of the natural, without necessarily needing to have coherence between subjective theism/agnosticism and objective functional atheism. I think Charles Darwin was probably of this type. This stance arises out of a vigorous sense of truthfulness in relation to what seemed knowable by reliable observation and a logical natural explanation. I separate progressives out from conservatives not on the basis of whether they are of a boat-rocking or non-boat-rocking disposition but on the basis of where their final commitments lie in relation to the question of divinity and nature. Darwin, I suspect, is of a dispositionally conservative nature, but the degree of incoherence he could maintain between not wanting to offend established religion and finding even liberal Unitarian doctrines hard to believe, on the one hand, and his rigorous commitment to scientific positivism on the other hand, puts him in the progressive rather than the conservative party. He is committed to scientific truth, defined in naturalistic terms. He is not able to be finally committed to any definite theological stance.

Progressive 2 (P2) types reject the divine, see nature in materialist terms, and debunk religion as superstition and a cover for power, oppression, and the preservation of backward-looking social influence. This approach was not that common in the nineteenth century, but our Bertrand Russell types—definitely a P2—were formed in the tacit progressive scientism of the late nineteenth century.

To reiterate, after 1859 the long swing of Western academic culture from at least a nominally Christian to a functionally post-Christian set of cosmological, teleological, ethical, and metaphysical bearings, was largely complete. By the 1860s the progressive spirit of the nineteenth century on the Continent held that Kant's vision of the Enlightenment of Mankind by the torch formed out of the fusing of rationalist mathematical reason with empirical scientific truth was imminent. This pure and clean light had nothing to do with the darkness of religious superstition or mystical metaphysics, such that the real meaning of religion and philosophy (if they had any positive value at all) was moral and political. Pragmatism, positivism, and utilitarianism were developing strongly in the Anglo-American arena at this time, again, with an attitude of tacit methodological agnosticism as regards the nature and existence of God, though with a keen psychological and sociological interest in religious experience. Interestingly, it is in the latter half of the nineteenth century that the term "scientist" is invented, and that the notion of a war between science and religion is first put forward.[9] Only at this time does secular science comes to play a functionally theological role as a competitor to religion.[10] By the 1860s the study of society by positivistic and pragmatic lights was moving ahead powerfully. Only the ghost of Kierkegaard's 1840s musings prophesied that the Titanic of modern social theory would sink. He was right.

9. Key historical texts here are Draper, *History of the Conflict between Religion and Science*, (1874) and White, *The Warfare of Science with Theology in Christendom* (1894).

10. See Harrison, *The Territories of Science and Religion*.

4

Religion and Social Theory
Reconsidered

THE PASSAGE FROM KANT to Marx is both a momentous transition and entirely unsurprising. Excluding any substantive knowledge of "things in themselves"—to Kant, we only know our own experiences as made comprehensible by the *a priori* categories of our minds—effectively replaces metaphysics with epistemology by making the world revolve around the knowing subject.

Kant famously proposes:

> Let us then make the experiment whether we may not be more successful in metaphysics, if we assume that objects must conform to our knowledge. . . . [W]e here propose to do just what Copernicus did in attempting to explain the celestial movements . . . .[1]

Once Kantian epistemic anthropocentrism is accepted one can easily keep the human subject at the center of our knowable universe and replace transcendental or idealist reason with the existing subject's concrete and materially concerned actions (praxis).

1. Kant, *Critique of Pure Reason*, 15.

Marx, accepting Feuerbach's reduction of religion to anthropology, uses Kant's same analogy of an anthropocentric formulation of Copernican cosmology:

> The criticism of religion disillusions man so that he will
> . . . [regain] his reason; so that he will revolve around
> himself as his own true sun.[2]

It is only a small and reasonable step from denying that the categories of human knowledge can know anything about God, to denying both God and faith entirely for those who would maintain respect for reasonable (that is modern anthropocentric) knowledge.[3] And if fearless critique is set up by Kant to combat skepticism and to sure up rational morality, there is no reason why critique itself cannot harden into a universal attack on "everything established"—including abstract reason and rational morality.[4]

Yet, between Kant and Marx there is Hegel. Here historical contextual evolution claims to re-connect the thing in itself with the human mind's capacity to reason. Thus, pure reason gives us Spirit within history; yet if pure reason is—as Schelling seems to maintain—always on the side of essence and unable to reach existence, then actual contextual interpretation tied to the physical conditions upon which culture depends can be freed from Hegel's impossible attempt to overcome Kant by sheer abstract thinking. Ignoring the subterfuge and illusion of high reasoning and religious conviction, Marx sees the material realities that are served by doctrine, ideology, and mythology and locates the importance

2. From Karl Marx, "Contribution to the Critique of Hegel's Philosophy of Right: Introduction," 1843. Tucker, *The Marx-Engels Reader*, 55.

3. Kant, *Critique of Pure Reason*, Bxxx ". . . in relation to the concept of God . . . speculative reason . . . must make use of principles which, in fact, extend only to the objects of possible experience, and which cannot be applied to objects beyond this sphere. . . . I must therefore abolish knowledge to make room for faith." See Karl Marx, "Contribution to the Critique of Hegel's Philosophy of Right: Introduction," "Theses on Feuerbach," in Tucker, *The Marx-Engels Reader*, 53–65, 143–45.

4. In Marx's letter to Arnold Ruge in September of 1843 he revels in the destructive power of "the unrestrained criticism of everything established." As cited in Desmond, *The Intimate Strangeness of Being*, 99n10.

of shared beliefs in relation to how people act and what relations of power they uphold over the means of material production. While Marx is a highly subtle and penetrating thinker, it is the uncompromising boldness of his vision, where he sees everything through the lens of material and power-focused action, that enables him to extract useful things from Kant and Hegel and move entirely beyond philosophy as such to the politics of materialism. Yet, this movement is indeed possible, even invited, by what Kant and Hegel did before him.

As mentioned, Kierkegaard's intellectual world was profoundly shaped by Kant and Hegel, and he knew the trajectories of Strauss and Feuerbach well. Indeed, reading Kierkegaard, Marx, and Nietzsche in parallel on the relationship between the burgher capitalist life-form and the Christian religion within that life-form, it is hard to miss the fact that they share the same larger intellectual landscape. And yet to isolate Kierkegaard, his interpretation of why things are as they are and his understanding of that which is causal and that which is derivative is diametrically at odds with Marx and Nietzsche.

If we are to consider whether Kierkegaard's critique of the public and the press in the Present Age—in our age—is valid or not, some very basic interpretive questions will need to be raised about the relationship between religion and society. Is religion straightforwardly derivative of material necessities and practical actions, as Marx maintains, or is the picture more complex? Significantly, within sociology, Max Weber maintains that religion can be causal of material structures, but this stance is put forward within a firmly agnostic view (which is to say, a methodologically and functionally atheist outlook) as regards the object of religious devotion (the Divine). In the final analysis, Weber is nuancing Marx on religion rather than offering a radical alternative to Marx. But Kierkegaard is radical; here the passion (or absence) of faith is causal of the social, political, and pragmatic features of any given life-world. To Kierkegaard the very subjectivity of faith is a marker of its truth, rather than locating it as an interpretive gloss on an objectively positive, external, material world of practical action.[5]

EITHER INWARDNESS AND UPWARDNESS OR PURE EXTERNALITY

The relationship between inwardness and upwardness in Kierkegaaard is straightforwardly Augustinian. That is, God—as the immediate grounds of being in (yet beyond) all beings—is closer to the soul than the ego, hence inwardness is the realm of contact with transcendence. Or in Kierkegaard's parlance, inwardness is where the soul contacts that which is primitive. The soul's being is derived from the continuous creative relationship between it and God—the soul is not a self-generating entity—and where there is alienation between the "I" and God then the soul turns to external concerns and either builds false transcendences out of the traces of God that tantalize immanence, or neglects transcendence (and its own grounds) entirely, replacing truth and meaning with external necessity and mere sensuality.

Kierkegaard's analysis of sin in *The Sickness Unto Death* is a function of his Augustinian psychic taxonomy. Because the self is a relation that relates inwardly to itself, this is a relation chronically prone to the spiritual pathology of trying to establish its own identity out of the categories of self-worship (despair). Yet, ironically, to do this the soul must look for reflections of itself in externalities, for inwardness without awareness of transcendence grounding the soul cannot define the soul. Thus, fabrications of a

5. Kierkegaard does not doubt the reality of the *external* world, but he strongly resists the idea that you can objectively prove or scientifically demonstrate anything that is really crucial for the soul's relation to God. Everything of real importance—from where we sit—happens in the secrecy of subjectivity, between the soul and God. Unlike the historical-critical thinkers of Kierkegaard's day, such as David Strauss, Kierkegaard had no doubt that Christ was a historical figure who lived, was crucified, and rose from the dead in first-century Palestine. But that historical truth remains a *mere external fact*, that, *in itself*, will save no soul. It is the *internal relation of the soul to God* wherein the primary existential truth of salvation resides.

functional inner identity can be built out of self-reflections that arise in cultural contexts and in relation to the physical necessities of lived existence. Yet such identity-constructions cannot generate a source of non-contingent truth and intrinsic meaning within the soul's own inwardness by herself. So every externally mediated object that is a mirror for self-worship fails to relate the soul to her genuine source of being, a source that is beyond the ego and that no external mediation can produce. That is, sin is an inner psychic pathology that is a misrelation of the ego to the ontic grounds of its own existence. This misrelation is what the Christian tradition calls death. The Christian tradition also maintains that we are all thrown into the world where we are born with this sickness unto death. Sin is there within us from the very beginning—sin is not something we *do*, it is within who we *are*. And yet, the Christian gospel is that Christ has conquered death and by the passion of faith we can cleave to his life and find a true relation back to the source of spiritual life, which is the wellspring of our own soul. The living soul—the soul that has life, freedom, joy, knows true meaning, and participates in the creative richness of the Creator welling up from within—draws its life not from the oh-so-contingent, oh-so-transient externally provided materials out of which it can build idols of itself to try and construct ultimacy for a few short years, but finds transcendent reaching down within the immanence of its own inwardness.

In Augustinian terms, the wondrous yet spluttering history of human culture—with all its pathos of beauty and banality, glory and shame, love and hatred, tenderness and brutality—is a function of the pathologies of idolatrous self-love; the vain attempt to find meaning and generate glory in a world overshadowed by the ontological mockery of death. Yet the community of those who seek to live in the life of God is located within the larger world of idolatry, as a site of redemption for the world. This is true even though the church is a community of sinners where the psychic illness that characterizes the world is found in abundance within the church. The crucial difference between the church and the world is that the church exists to *treat*, rather than admire, the illness of sin.

Any reading of *The City of God* illustrates that the relation of the church to the world is one that considerably exercised Augustine. Likewise, Kierkegaard is continuously grappling with this relationship. For should the self-love and idolatrous pagan infatuation with externalities characteristic of the world overly colonize the norms of the church, then the church becomes the site of the bleakest of all hopelessness and the spiritual life-spring of Western culture must dry up. Kierkegaard was convinced that the degree of colonization of the Danish Church in his times was so high that success in the hierarchy of the church almost presupposed an absence of inwardness and a denial of the inner life-source of the gospel. Thus, when the church becomes paradigmatically illustrative of the absence of inwardness characteristic of the Present Age then the very idea of transcendence becomes unintelligible and banality in religion denies the validity of transcendence itself. For this reason Kierkegaard found much he could recognize as valid in Feuerbach's *Essence of Christianity*.[6] Or, as a saying of Jesus puts it, the followers of Christ are called to be the salt and light of the world;[7] they are charged with preserving the good in the world, with giving the flavor of life to the world, with illuminating the true source of life in such a manner that the idolatries of the age are seen as shallow and degrading in comparison.[8] But if the salt

6. See Malantschuk, *The Controversial Kierkegaard*, 76–82.

7. Matt 5:13–16.

8. Note, Kierkegaard does not think that only dogmatically orthodox Christians can be true followers of Christ. Indeed, there is no necessary relationship between the external signs of belonging to a Christian religious institution and being an actual follower of Christ (i.e., walking in his outcast and extraordinary way). Rather the necessary relationship is in the "how" of inwardness, rather than the "what" of doctrine—even though the "what" of doctrine is not unimportant. See Kierkegaard, *Concluding Unscientific Postscript*, 201: "If someone who lives in the midst of Christianity enters, with knowledge of the true idea of God, the house of God, the house of the true God, and prays, but prays in untruth, and if someone lives in an idolatrous land but prays with all the passion of infinity, although his eyes are resting on the image of an idol—where then is the more truth? The one prays in truth to God although he worships an idol; the other prays in untruth to the true God and is therefore in truth worshipping an idol."

loses its savor and if the light in the church becomes darkness, then the world only has the empty idolatry of mere externality, and lives ever in the grip of the fates under the final lordship of death. Thus, a church without inner life is worthless and must be thrown out and trampled underfoot.

It is because Kierkegaard loved the church and the world that he so forthrightly attacked the worldliness of the church. He did not want the church to be thrown out and trampled underfoot, and he did not want the world to be without a believable witness to genuine religious truth. For in the West, the world without Christian witness is cut off from its religious heritage and thus bereft of any high spiritual grounds to give life to culture, substantial value to morality, and meaning to ambition. Kierkegaard saw clearly that the post-Christian West will only have the transience, relativity, and externality of mere material immediacy out of which to construct individual identity, and thus all meanings and human being itself will be mere artful illusions that no one believes, drawn from the limited materials available to a cultural imagination that has no belief in transcendence. Due to science, this post-Christian age may well be more instrumentally potent than any previous age, and may have more material niceties than any previous age, but the fruits of this technology will all be external distractions hiding a vast inner emptiness, giving the soul of the age no horizon of transcendence from which to orientate its meanings and values. All—in the final despairing analysis—will seem garrulous. Interestingly, outside of Kierkegaard it is Nietzsche who most keenly appreciates what the death of God in Western culture means for the burgher class.[9] On how lost the "small man" is in an age without God, Nietzsche and Kierkegaard speak with one voice.

---

9. Friedrich Nietzsche: "He who does not finds greatness in God finds it nowhere. He must either deny it or create it." As cited by Tanner, *Nietzsche*, 42. It is also interesting to note that both Kierkegaard and Nietzsche see the nihilism of the Present Age as offering a remarkable opportunity to those individuals who refuse to be defined by that age. Of course, the opportunities envisioned by Nietzsche and Kierkegaard are polar opposites. To Kierkegaard the hunger for any taste of life will force the seeker to abandon the dead religious props of Christendom and will drive the seeker inwards where they will

If an Augustinian psychology is true, then the most significant causal factors in all human worlds is the health or sickness of the inward relation to the upward in the individual. This is not to say that inwardness and upwardness are ever merely individual attainments. Not at all—for each acting and reacting individual is situated in relationships with other individuals, and with collectives of different forms, and thinks and moves within the gifts of language and culture that are the contingencies and spatio-temporal specificities of the actual concrete existence of any individual. Even so, there is an irreducible inner sanctum in each soul—so Augustine maintains—that can be filled and enlivened by nothing other than God.[10] Here, religion as a function of human inwardness, relates the soul to God, linking immanence with transcendence, and is thereby the spiritual life-spring of human culture. Thus culture, meaning, and value are both immanently (yet derivatively) *made by* humans and also *given to* humanity from beyond itself. Here God is the most basic reality defining meaning, value, and spirit in the human world.

It is necessary to point this out, because there can be no middle ground on this matter. Secular modernity's bracketing of God and of the inner realm of contact with transcendence out of the public and knowable realm of practical reality is not an option. Secular modernity performs this bracketing so that we can have a functionally materialist, functionally atheist intellectual culture while still respecting people's freedom to believe in God if they so choose.[11] In fact, the vision of the world that such a bracketing offers is a world where all that is most primary to a living faith is made entirely invisible. No, either one does not believe in the

find God. To Nietzsche, the *Übermensch* will realize there is no meaning other than what we create, and will not let anyone else manufacture meaning for him, but will generate his own greatness out of his own will to truth, his own will to power, his own animal vitality of immediate and material life.

10. Augustine, *The Confessions of Saint Augustine*, 15: "you made us for yourself, and our heart is restless until it finds rest in you."

11. There is something very refreshing in the evangelical scientist atheism of Richard Dawkins, Christopher Hitchens, and Daniel Dennett. Where the externally measurable objects of natural science are alone taken as real, this then excludes the possibility of transcendence entirely.

soul and God and (if it were possible) is honest about what that means,[12] or one does believe in the soul and God and situates one's understanding of culture and matter relative to that primary belief.

So we must make a choice. On the one hand, there is militant materialism where there is no transcendent God and all meanings, all morality, all purposes are constructed out of nothing other than sheer will and imagination. This does indeed involve—as Marx saw—the "unrestrained criticism of all things established," where all traces of the soul, of God, and of transcendence must be purged from our heritage. Matter and power alone are real. Here meaning is a fabrication, morality is a fabrication, identities are fabrications, and all human achievements and relationships carry no transcendent cargo. Or—on the other hand—there is God and the human soul. This is Kierkegaard's stance. Here all thinking about culture, economics, politics, the media, etc., must be framed entirely through the lens of the soul and God, as the primary and governing realities of the world of human existence.

PLATO

The most pointed, and still possibly the most powerful defense of the validity of Kierkegaard's outlook was put forward at the dawn of the West's high intellectual heritage by Plato;[13] and indeed—as Nietzsche correctly noticed—Christianity, and hence Augustine and Kierkegaard, sit within this aspect of the Platonist tradition of the West.[14] Essentially, Plato argues that if there is no intrinsic qualitative reality that eternally is, then transience and flux are the only realities, and then intelligibility is not possible as there is

---

12. If the Augustinian outlook is true then it is not possible to believe in the reality of pure immanence honestly. That is, self-deception is essential to believing in pure immanence if Augustine is right. To honestly believe that meaning, purpose, value, and spirit can be constructed over the top of meaningless, purposeless, valueless, material imminence is to believe that all that is existentially significant is fictional. This, actually, cannot be honestly done.

13. Plato, *Republic*, book 2, book 6 & 7; Plato, *The Sophist*.

14. Nietzsche, *Beyond Good and Evil*, x.

nothing enduringly there that one could know and all the tools of our thinking and speaking and all the values that guide our actions are also entirely contingent and transient, and thus truth-seeking reasoning itself is an impossible exercise. That is, philosophy itself would be impossible were this true, and were this true then there can be no *argument* in support of a metaphysics that assumes that reality as we know it is mere materiality embedded in flux and contingency and all values are fundamentally relative. If one is going to reason at all—if, existentially, one is to take reasoning and meaning as primary human realities—then one must believe in the grounds of reality being other than merely contingent, merely in flux, and merely "there" without value or meaning. That is, to believe in a merely material reality one must simply irrationally *assert* that it is thus and simply irrationally *assert* that rationality itself is ontologically delusional. If this is the case then reasoning is simply violence by other means, and violence goes all the way down in reality. But here, that one even seeks to communicate a negative *meaning* as *true*—maintaining that all views of reality *really* are contingent, and only those views that know they are contingent illusions can be taken to be honestly false—belies the existence of a soul that reasons about truth and that attempts to communicate real meanings (however contingently mediated and relatively situated). Thus, the ancients held that mind and meaning and eternal being were prior to existential becoming, contingent knowing, and ontologically derivative material flux. Indeed, *Logos* must be taken as ontologically prior to contingent and spatio-temporally embedded perception if one is to consider perception meaningful, contingency comprehensible, and flux observable by virtue of its relation to some order of reality that is not in flux.[15] That is, the flux

15. Gerson, *Ancient Epistemology*, 25 "Aristotle (following Plato) will argue that it is not possible to understand what we sense, though it is possible to understand the intelligible structure of what we sense. To adduce theoretically sensible, albeit practically non-sensible, things as constituting the explanations for the order in nature is to abandon the possibility of explanation or understanding altogether." That is, it was taken as obvious that intelligence in the knower and intelligibility in the cosmos is the precondition for meaningful sensation. That is, the ancients typically assumed the primacy of intrinsic

and contingency of our immediate experience is only recognizable as flux and contingency because there is something within us as knowers and something behind the apparent cosmos that does not change and that is not contingent.

How anything *could* be understood, how any knowing soul *could* think, how communication *could* have any meaning at all in an entirely materialist cosmos, governed entirely by spatio-temporal flux, is not at all clear. Philosophically—that is, from an existential stance committed to reason and meaning—the onus of proof is on those who want to maintain that our immediate and onto-epistemologically primary embeddedness in meaning, value, and reason could be comprehensibly taken to be an illusion. That is, belief in a merely materialist cosmos that has no frame of meaning, no grounding in reason, no intrinsic value is a doctrine that could not be demonstrated, for the very idea of demonstration relies on the reality of the things such a doctrine denies reality to.

The fact is that modernity has abandoned the ancient Neoplatonist wisdom tradition of the West, where divinity, value, thought, and meaning are primary and where contingent matter embedded in the spatio-temporal manifold is a derivative property of ontic reality. Even so, the story of that abandonment is not the story of the *philosophical* triumph of materialism.[16] Rather, this

meaning over contingent knowing. More broadly, Gerson's text is a very interesting argument for the ongoing vitality of the ancient priority of cosmic meaning over specific human knowing. Indeed, after reading Gerson, I cannot see how the post-Kantian view—where a *natura pura* ratio-empirical modern understanding of human knowing is the foundation of truth and meaning, purely within the ontologically isolated consciousness of the individual mind—*could* be made to work.

16. Note, that modern rationalist and empiricist metaphysics has failed does not mean that materialist metaphysics has succeeded. Rather, metaphysics itself has been abandoned in the wake of the failures of rationalist and empiricist metaphysics and as a result of Kant's bold attempt to replace metaphysics with epistemology. This has made it possible to hold fundamentally untenable metaphysical stances while all the while claiming we do not have a metaphysics, or that metaphysics is simply a branch of physics. William Desmond's work (see *The Intimate Strangeness of Being*) gives persuasive argument to the case that not only was the abandonment of metaphysics by Kant an over-reaction to the distinctive forms of metaphysical impossibility he was seeking to address,

is the story of the *practical* triumph of modern science and the *political* triumph of modern secularism. Both modern science and modern secularism as powerful governing principles within the modern life-form set up a legal fiction that separates facts from values, meaning from information, thought from knowledge, being from doing. These artificial separations make it possible for us to lopsidedly equate facts, information, knowledge, and doing with objective truth and public intellectual pursuits, and to equate values, meaning, thought, and being with subjective fantasies and private opinions. This set-up allows us to have whatever values we like, whatever beliefs about reality that our subjective taste finds palatable, and lets us do whatever we practically *can* do without having to concern ourselves with the question of whether our actions are good or evil. Though, to our liberal, pragmatic Present Age, we must consider whether our actions are legal or illegal.

For our dominant men of action, modernity is a very convenient set-up really, perfectly suited to the entirely externally focused Present Age that Kierkegaard describes. In this context it is unsurprising to see how the simply asserted materialism of Marx and his sophisticated replacement of philosophy with politics and economics had such a ready take up in the early decades of the social sciences.

I cannot see how a materialism of pure immanence could in any way carry real meaning. That is, materialism cannot be a serious philosophical doctrine for philosophy presupposes cosmic meaning. A materialism of pure immanence denies cosmic meaning and is committed to "meaning" as a meaningless artifice of non-rational, non-qualitative mere mater and energy; everything reduces to irrational contingent necessity and the power or absence of power to pursue "interests" which are defined by nothing other than irrational contingent necessity. This is why political

---

but that the idea that we actually *can* simply avoid metaphysics is untenable. Desmond's work powerfully suggests that we do not have a choice between having a metaphysics or not having one; rather our choice is between pursuing a credible and subtle metaphysics that makes some analogical contact with reality or of uncritically simply assuming an incredible and crude metaphysics that is merely a function of how we pragmatically want to see the world.

and economic praxis, assuming methodological atheism, is put forward by Marx as an *alternative* to philosophy;[17] practical materialism repudiates cosmic rationality and essential meaning.

FORGET MATERIALISM—SO WHERE TO FROM HERE?

It is clear why no philosophical defense is offered for reductive pragmatic materialism; a cosmos embedded in continuous temporal transition such as ours cannot sustain any argument for having no frame of meaning beyond transience without philosophical self-destruction. The type of social science based analysis of politics, economics, and society, and the scientistic understanding of the soul characteristic of post-Freudian psychology have all abandoned philosophy and all expect us to replace human freedom and meaning with necessary, manipulative, and mechanistic power in how we understand such things as the press and the public. But in this little book, I will take it as undemonstrated (even indemonstrable) that philosophy has been superseded by science and politics, that becoming has no dependence on being, and that the divisions of secular modernity are anything other than convenient legal fictions maintained and assumed because they suit an age without any shared appreciation of inwardness and upwardness. So from this point forward we will not seriously consider the outlook on society and the relation of the individual to society that has no appreciation for the spiritual dynamics of the relation of the soul to God. Kierkegaard's theologically grounded approach to sociology, simply in virtue of it being theological, has an astonishing advantage over methodologically atheist accounts of human behavior. Indeed, I would suggest that a theological grounding to sociology is the only viable form of social theory. Kierkegaard's approach is valuable precisely because it did not follow the main direction of the social sciences from the 1840s to the mid-twentieth century.

17. See Marx, "Theses on Feuerbach," in Tucker, *The Marx-Engels Reader*, 143–45, ending with the famous thesis XI: "The philosophers have only interpreted the world, in various ways; the point, however, is to change it."

5

Kierkegaard's Theological Sociology of the Present Age

KIERKEGAARD'S UNDERSTANDING OF THE interdependent relationship between inwardness, existential practice, and socio-cultural norms leads him to discern a distinctive trajectory for the Present Age. Given what he saw as the widespread failure of religious inwardness in the increasingly powerful burgher class of Europe in the 1840s he foresaw a corresponding retreat of upwardness from the normative cultural perspective of the age, which would result in the reduction of the meaning horizons of social reality to mere externalities. This in turn produces the most spiritually oppressive levelling because no inner distinctive could be even recognized where the dominant interpretive frame of the age is focused entirely on externalities. Thus, individuals define their own identity as reflections of the cipher of statistical normality produced by the mindless and spiritless homogeneity of the herd, of the masses, of the public. This soulless public protects and advances itself—maintaining a culture of spiritual poverty—through the press. No-one drives the press, it is rather a function of the type of collective consciousness of massified, relatively wealthy, and increasingly atomized individuals who are non-the-less homogenized and spiritually impoverished.

Jacques Ellul takes Kierkegaard's perspective up in the twentieth century.[1] We now live in a technological society that is characterized by the sacrifice of all substantive and intrinsic *ends* to the improvement of instrumental *means*. It is not that technology is either problematic or optional in itself, rather it is because we have no spiritual vision of substantive ends that mere physical externalities and socio-biological necessities determine the only ends that have any meaning in our culture. That is, what Ellul calls *la technique* is a form of cultural consciousness where an obsession with instrumental power and efficiency occludes any real consideration of substantive ends and intrinsic values.[2] Under this form of cultural consciousness the state grows in its regulation and facilitation of merely material and merely socio-biologically necessary ends, and all values and meanings are effectively privatized and withdrawn from the increasingly technocratic spheres of national, public, and commercial rational interests and action. Administration, management, and publicity become things in their own right and thus large bureaucracies generate enormous self-contained worlds of procedural and public relations such that the means of institutional operation become ends in themselves. More broadly, in a culture shaped by no shared vision of intrinsic meaning, one now lives simply in order to eat, to work, to be healthy, to gain wealth, security, skills, knowledge, entertainment, satiation; one does not understand the idea of eating, working, acquiring

1. Ellul, *The Technological Society*, 55: "In the mid nineteenth century, when technique had hardly begun to develop, a voice was raised in prophetic warning against it. The voice was Kierkegaard's. But his warnings, solidly thought out though they were, and in the strongest sense of the word prophetic, were not heeded. . . . They were too close to the truth." Ellul opens his *The Subversion of Christianity* with a bracing quote from Kierkegaard's *The Instant*. Ellul read Kierkegaard closely and found in him not only a theological and philosophical voice of great power, but equally a socio-cultural and psychological understanding that he was in remarkable sympathy with.

2. Note: "Ellul does not argue against technique or technology itself, but rather [he is against] the human mindset that replaces critical moral discourse with technological means and values." Randolph Kluver, "Jacques Ellul: Technique, Propaganda, and Modern Media," chapter 4 in Lum (ed.), *Perspectives on Culture, Technology and Communication*, 99.

money, etc., as a means to any substantive qualitative vision of living. Max Weber's understanding of the purely procedural logic of formal bureaucratic intelligence and the manner in which large institutions gain a governing ethos, which in its very efficiency and instrumental effectiveness becomes radically inhuman, is also an important influence on Ellul's thought. That is, we now live in a massified society where technology is not just a matter of applying science in order to solve practical problems, but is a political, organizational, and economic principle governing, homogenizing, and de-humanizing every aspect of society.

This brings us to propaganda.[3] By "propaganda" Ellul means the total information-, attitude-, feeling-, and opinion-environment in which the person who lives in the modern mass culture of the technological society is fully immersed. That is, propaganda is necessary and ubiquitous in the technological society. It is necessary because there is no collective spiritual medium of communion in which the individuals of functional materialism can consciously know each other as souls. Without an awareness of spiritual communion, there is no language available for spiritually meaningful communication. Thus, information replaces communication just as the techniques of mass media manipulation replace any meaningful practice of participatory politics. This age is, as Kierkegaard put it, an age of publicity and of superficial and immediate reflections. In this age, what Ellul understands by the term propaganda is a necessary continuous background noise assuring us that our atomized, alienated, spiritually empty, morally compromised, and aimless lives make us genuinely happy and fulfilled.

But, of course, our consumer life-world does not make us happy and fulfilled. Although we have anything that money can buy we have nothing that it cannot buy, such as dignity, purpose, love, and meaning. Instead, we have anomia, despair, mental health issues, relentless activity, profound loneliness, fear, and anger. The kind of understanding of the real nature of modern society that Kierkegaard and Ellul enable is simply not accessible to a methodologically atheistic and metaphysically materialist social science.

3. See Ellul, *Propaganda*.

But, as we have seen, such social science is incoherent and self-defeating. We are not obliged to accept it as it stands. Could we imagine a different way of understanding and living in our social worlds? Could things be different in both our understanding and our lived reality?

THE FUTURE OF THE PRESENT AGE

Interestingly, the analyses Kierkegaard and Ellul put forward about the Present Age usually strikes the social scientific ear as being remarkably bleak, but this is not so. That they offer no technical, ideological, or sociological solution to the levelling power of the public and the pervasive banalizing and sedative power of the mass media is essential to their message; for that would be to perpetuate the problem.[4] The core of the problem—as Ellul and Kierkegaard see it—is spiritual. And here also is the core of redemptive hope and the reason why a negative trajectory simply cannot keep on getting worse forever.

If it is true that the individual is primarily an individual because she is ontically grounded in God, then this age's attempt to construct society without reference to this reality means this civilizational pathway cannot actually succeed. That is, the mass propagated operational convictions of our age—that the individual is *self*-grounded, that materiality, externality, and instrumental power alone are real, and that meanings, purposes, and values are entirely poetically constructed with no grounding in transcendence—are a bizarre delusion that cannot ultimately be believed or culturally sustained. Indeed, the religious inadequacy of this age is reflected in the staggering need for meaning and fulfillment our entertainment industry seeks to fill by generating an ocean

---

4. Unsurprisingly, to those who do not share Ellul's understanding of the centrality of transcendence and the soul in human affairs, Ellul is readily seen as expounding the most savage "technological pessimism." Thus, Gomez claims that "Jacques Ellul . . . is the most extreme representative of . . . technological determinism bordering on fatalism." ["What Is This Thing Called Philosophy of Technology?" www.eolss.net/Sample-Chapters/C05/E6-89-23-00.pdf, 8.]

of low-level pagan mythologies out of sex, violent power, and the paranormal.[5] The deeply culturally penetrating technologies of theatre (and advertising is at the core of this theatre) in our age display to us the fantasies compatible with our functional materialism, and they work very hard, with enormous creativity and staggering resources to generate images of meaning for us to worship out of things that simply cannot carry meaning in themselves. This type of mythology is central to the modern age, particularly in the tropes and themes of soulless glory and merely voyeuristic significance portrayed to us via our Olympians—actors and celebrities. But our gods are just the banal spiritually petty projections of the bland cipher that is the mass-society "man"; a cipher constructed in the image of his merely sensual, merely material, merely instrumental, power-centric imagination. There is no spiritual meat here capable of sustaining a civilization.

The Augustinian outlook is that evil is an absence and a perversion of reality and Kierkegaard likewise understands sin as an impossible attempt at the mis-relation of the soul to its fundamental source and destiny rather than any act or thing of any substantive reality. Evil and sin and soullessness cannot, finally, work. And they do not in fact work. As blind as we may be to where real meaning can be found, it still finds us even in the technological society saturated with its omnipresent propaganda. We can try to create hell on earth, and broadcast the merely sensual dream of our own eschaton over the top of it, yet our creation is—blessedly—ever

---

5. I here use the term "religious" as Kierkegaard uses it in *Two Ages* (concerning the relation of the soul to God), and the term "pagan" as Kierkegaard uses it in *Concluding Unscientific Postscript* (defining spirit in the terms of direct and external recognition). Interestingly, Peter Berger well understood the manner in which the "supernatural" is the pornography of the modern mind, and the manner in which sexuality is sacralized and made to carry an enormous burden of existential meaning in our times. See Berger, *Facing Up to Modernity*, chapter 17, "The Devil and the Pornography of the Modern Mind" and chapter 16, "Cakes for the Queen of Heaven; 2,500 years of Religious Ecstasy." Walter Wink, following Paul Ricoeur, also notices how the myth of redemptive violence and an essentially Babylonian cosmology of original violence is deeply ingrained in our very impotent and unredeemed lives. See Wink, *Engaging the Powers*, 13–32.

so religiously shitty, and our impossible externally referenced desire/satisfaction dream, even where we believe it, does not in fact obliterate waking life. For these reasons the Present Age, sooner or later, will end up with a culture defined by near complete spiritual implosion and die at its own hands.

My guess is that in the next century the global world order as we know it will have gone the way of all imperial civilizations that run out of spiritual dynamism and the next constructive civilizational spirituality will be given to the world from either Islam, non-Western Christianity, or from some new religious consciousness—possibly coming from China or India. On the other hand, it is certainly possible that demonic and idolatrous mass spiritualities will arise to fill the religious vacuum generated by today's global consumerism. Yet positively or negatively, sooner or later, the religious imperatives of the human soul demand that the spiritual vacuum of late modern Western consumerism must be filled. The Present Age is not culturally sustainable in terms of the religious vision it needs in order to give its civilization values and meanings worthy of the human soul. This age will pass as one of the oft-repeated civilizational trajectories of human history: a civilization that starts out with a dynamism and creative drive wrought of its religious vitality rises to power and prosperity and then develops, over time, into a merely pragmatic civilization that tries to run without spiritual fuel or any higher guiding vision. We are now like Atlantis just before the rising of the sea; we have extraordinary magical powers, wondrous manipulative knowledge, we are structurally embedded in exploitative immorality regarding the human and natural resources that make our life-form possible, and our centers of power are ingrained in a hubristic folly and a tragic spiritual poverty, which means we will not draw back from the brink of destruction. All cataclysmic collapses are horrendous, but really, the sooner the end of this age comes, the better.

But what can we do now? How can a theologically situated understanding of the Present Age inform the vision and practice of a Christian witness both within and to our times?

PART TWO

Taking Theology Seriously
—Sociologically

In Part One of this book we have explored Kierkegaard's doxological understanding of the individual within society. We have also touched on why it seems strange to the prevailing outlook of our times to think of society in anything other than materialist and functionally atheistic terms. Even so, sociological materialism is, for many reasons, hard to believe, even to the perspectives native to secular modernity. More seriously, such an outlook is a denial of a Christian understanding of what it means to be an individual before God, and what it means to live in good relations with others.

As yet, we have not drawn out this obvious implication of Kierkegaard's *Two Ages*: a Christian sociological perspective cannot accept a materialist outlook. And yet, the collectively affirmed fictions of secularism and the functionally atheistic assumptions of our knowledge and power culture—deep features of our sociological life-world—define the social reality in which we actually live.[1] This describes a situation that is very dangerous for modern Western Christians. This describes a situation where—in Augustine's terms—the City of Man sets the tacit operational terms in which

1. Concerning how social reality works, see Berger and Luckmann, *The Social Construction of Reality*.

61

the City of God must function. This is a particularly difficult situation for Protestant Evangelicals (like myself) for in many ways, it was we who created modern Western secularism.[2]

In Part One of this book I hope to have shown that the vision of who we are and what society is that Kierkegaard's doxologically framed sociology reveals is very perceptive. I think the case can be strongly made that Kierkegaard's theological sociology is stunningly more compatible with our actual experience of existence than is the functionally atheistic, metaphysically materialist, and progressive social science vision of reality. Kierkegaard shows us that a materialist social scientific perspective on God, the soul, and society is an abstract ideology that we are under no compelling intellectual or evidential obligation to believe. And yet we *do* (sociologically) believe it.

We believe in a functionally atheist, functionally materialist, secular society in our actions, in our conformity to the norms that govern our conventional interactions with others, in our conformity to the norms that govern the commerce, entertainment, workplace, civic, and administrative dynamics in which we participate. Believing is here an existential term. That is, existential belief here is something manifest in habitual and assumed practices. Looking at belief in social practice is the litmus test illustrating what our most fundamental lived loyalties and enacted commitments really are.

Thinking about belief in this way is entirely biblical. In John's Gospel "belief" is a verb, it is a "believing in" as an action of trust, an abiding in the meaning and reality of a distinctive way of life (John 6:29; 8:31–32), a set of life-form reflexes shared in common with the community of believers to which we belong. And we always belong to a community of believers who believe in one way of life or another.

I hope you will not find this melodramatic, but when it became clear to me how much I too am a product of the secular, materialist, atheist life-world in which I live, I felt smitten in a similar way to the prophet Isaiah. Isaiah is a pious Hebrew, but—via an

2. See Gregory, *The Unintended Reformation.*

astonishing revelation—he finds that he has unclean lips because he lives among a people of unclean lips and shares their common way of life (Isa 6:5). We too are functional atheists and pragmatic materialists, because this is the social reality in which we actually live, however personally religious we may also be, however sincerely pious in our individual convictions and personal morality we may also be.

How then can we see and live differently? How can we seek to become more Christian both "in the separation of the religious individual before God in the responsibility of eternity" *and* as members of social institutions, communities, shared practices, and a larger world of cultural meanings and social, economic, and civic power-relations?

In the New Testament it seems clear that seeing in some ways comes first. The word for repent in the New Testament is *metanoia*—which means a change of mind. This change of mind comes first, and then, by patience, discipline, and collective formation over time, a change of way of life is affected. So Part One has been about vision, about how there are two ways of seeing the social world in which we live and move. There is a way blind to doxology, and a way alert to doxology. Part Two is about identifying specific features of our life-world that are embedded in a doxologically blind set of functionally materialist assumptions, and then seeking to re-think how we might address practices and formations for both individual Christians and the church that seeks to enable an alternative way of life to what is normative to our larger social life-world. The first chapter here is still quite theoretical—it is a chapter about knowledge. But knowledge understood sociologically is one of the most powerful, unnoticed background features of any given way of life, so we have to look at it closely in order to be realistically concrete in the last two chapters on money and religion.

In writing this section it has become clear to me that simply becoming aware of our doxological blind spots, in itself, does not overcome our functional blindness and habitual idolatry. The reason for this is sociologically obvious: we are *embedded* in a doxologically blind and idolatrous way of life. Even so, unless we first know we are blind idolaters, we will not seek for a sociological miracle; a new way of living in fellowship with God, the church, and the world that is not doxologically blind and misguided. So Part Two of this book is not so much of a how-to manual for a doxologically credible way of life, it is more of a spelling out of how deeply embedded we are in blind and false frames of lived worship. Moving out of that place will not happen because of some theoretical gnosis or the application of some technology of our own making, but the hope of all prophetic speech is that God himself will heal our sight and empower us with his life-breath if we can collectively repent and seek his face.

Kierkegaard has opened the way for us. Let us continue on from his analysis, taking up his central insight regarding doxology, and look more closely at the specific dynamics of *our* Present Age though that lens.

6

Knowledge

How does knowledge—both sociologically and theoretically—work as a broad social-reality structure undergirding secular modernity, in the modern Western university, and as the engine and guarantor of our technological society? What is the doxological topography of our knowledge?

We will explore knowledge under four headings. Let us look at how knowledge is a collective human activity, embedded in language, metaphysically entangled, and always theologically loaded and politically charged.

1. KNOWLEDGE IS A COLLECTIVE HUMAN ACTIVITY

This first point is quite general: sociologically, knowledge is always produced by communities of knowers. This is as true for the sciences as it is for the humanities, it is as true for the traditional Aboriginal knowledge of the night sky as it is for NASA astrophysicists using the Hubble telescope. In the late 1950s and early 1960s Michael Polanyi and Thomas Kuhn unpacked the complex ways in which scientific knowledge is always situated within communities of interpretation and practice, such that inspirations had and observations done by individual scientists are never simply their own discoveries.[1] Things have moved on in the field of the sociology of scientific knowledge since then, but the basic insights of the 1960s have been developed rather than discarded.

Even so, modern secular knowledge has an inbuilt resistance to acknowledging the innately communal nature of knowledge and interpretation. What we might call the doctrine of objectivity, combined with modernity's atomic "I," form us to think that there is nothing socially complex about knowledge. To our life-world, a true factual knowledge of reality can be had by any individual by a simple process of accurate *observation* and careful *reasoning*. This blindness to the social complexity of knowledge is neatly encapsulated in the truism that modern knowledge is reductive. The reductive outlook aims to filter out the quirkiness of immediate appearance and interpretive gloss, and the subjectivity of any affective, moral, or spiritual response in any recipient of sense dependent experience. The reductive gaze seeks to focus only on an observable, measurable, and mathematically modelable account of what is (in those terms) objectively there. The meaning of knowledge and the formation of knowers by communities of skill, interpretation, and methodological conformity, situated in time, place, language, and culture, need not be noticed to the reductive gaze.

Brad Gregory has pointed out that there is a religious history to this reductive outlook on knowledge. In a nutshell, Gregory argues that the splintering of Christendom after the Reformation tended to excise theology as much as possible from what was to become science, so that some functionally neutral territory between profoundly theologically combative communities of various Protestants, and of Protestants and Catholics, could talk to each other at all.[2] By the time Newton's *principia mathematica* appears, carefully measured observation and predictively verifiable

1. See Polanyi, *Personal Knowledge*; Kuhn, *The Structure of Scientific Revolutions*.

2. "An unintentional result of literally interminable, pervasive doctrinal controversy was a strong tendency towards the de facto elimination of substantive religious claims from any bearing on the investigation of the natural world." Gregory, *The Unintended Reformation*, 46–47.

mathematics provide a framework of objective and theologically disinterested knowledge that various creedal communities can understand in the terms of mathematics and measurement, whatever their interpretive gloss of Newton's work might be. The separation of facts from meanings, of knowers from the community of their interpretive formation, and of theology from science, has a European Christian heritage.

But, and it often takes a Roman Catholic to notice this, this neutrality was not actually metaphysically and theologically neutral at all. We will look more closely at this under the headings of metaphysics and theology below, but this needs to be briefly signposted here. Brad Gregory is a Roman Catholic and he points out that while the Catholic response to the Reformation and the post-Aristotelian natural philosophy of modernity was often far from admirable, and decidedly unhelpful, what was lost by the new objectivity was a sacramental understanding of reality grounded in a theology of God that was not univocal.[3] So observable real-

---

3. "Univocal" means "one meaning." This is a reductive linguistic tool that facilitates definitional clarity. Univocally, the word "bread" means *only* a physical, edible object made out of baked ground grain, and the word "wine" means *only* a liquid made from fermented grape juice. "Univocal" is the opposite of "equivocal" were the same word can have two entirely unconnected meanings. Such as a "pitcher" meaning either a jug of water or a baseball "pitcher" who throws a ball (and a picture on the wall of a pitcher throwing a ball at a pitcher, is both homophonic and equivocal). For definitional clarity all terms need to be rendered univocal by one means or another. The alternative to the univocal/equivocal dichotomy is *analogy*. Here "bread" can be like "the body of Christ" in some partial and suggestive manner. If one is a Roman Catholic then one combines analogy with sacramentality in the Eucharist such that the sanctified bread becomes the body of Christ through a spiritual participation, without ceasing to have all the tangible qualities of physical bread. So a strict insistence on univocity tends to find analogical meaning very problematic and renders sacramental thinking either "hocus pocus" nonsense, or a mystery totally exceeding rational comprehension. On this matter, it is worth pointing out that sacramental theology regarding what constituted a valid liturgical and ecclesiological participation in the Eucharist was a central site of ecclesial power struggles in sixteenth-century Europe. Matters of univocity, equivocity, and analogy in metaphysics and sacramental theology were (and remain) far from simply arcane points of definitional dispute. The distinctly Protestant push towards modernity tends to be non-analogical, and even—in many

ity comes to be understood as flatly material and entirely discrete from the supernatural such that God is effectively absented from nature. Religion is here understood to be entirely secondary to the physical nature of the real world. This is the historical context in which a modern, reductively objective knowledge of facts, and the separation of theology from natural philosophy, arises.

Another feature of the huge revolution in metaphysical assumptions in the seventeenth century was the Cartesian answer to skepticism; the cogito—"I think therefore I am." Descartes could not trust any external appearance (he might be dreaming, hallucinating, or being messed with by the devil), but he could not doubt that he himself existed as the site in which appearances were known. So Descartes thinks of his own soul as an unextended thinking substance that, alone of all things, cannot be doubted. This gives Descartes a firm foundation from which to build true knowledge. Reductive objectivity and the atomic "I" as the foundation of all valid knowledge—ironically—is the modern collective-formation context of our assumed cultural belief that collective formation in knowledge is not important. Combine this with the seventeenth-century metaphysical revolution Gassendi was producing[4]—this is the shift from Aristotelian metaphysics, where all beings are purposive integrations of matter and form, to the atomic materialism of Democritus—and we get meaningless material objectivity and atomic egoistic subjectivism bedding down in the very underpinnings of the modern mind's view a reality.

Then there is power. At the same time as Western Europe is finding it hard to believe in a sacramental and analogical theology of God and creation, the *point* of knowledge shifts from having a

non-conformists evangelicals—*anti*-sacramental, and this ratio-empirical definitionally clear (or, arguably, theologically and metaphysically impoverished) thinking is entangled in the Protestant influence on the Scientific Revolution of the seventeenth century. For this reason contemporary Christians who retain a high sacramental theology have a more natural suspicion of the metaphysical reductiveness of scientific modernity than do contemporary Christians who have abandoned a recognizably analogical and sacramental theology.

4. See Joy, *Gassendi the Atomist.*

doxological teleology to being *a means to power*, and being validated by its instrumental *use*.

Francis Bacon's *New Atlantis* is a seventeenth-century vision of a partially realized eschaton—the retrieval of humanity's God-given, pre-fallen sovereignty over nature—via science as technologically applied for the betterment of humanity.[5] Knowledge becomes power, power over nature in the service of the physical and governmental wellbeing of humanity.

The corollary of this knowledge-as-power view is that we measure how good our knowledge is by how powerfully effective its application is. It is true if it *works*. We will look more closely at knowledge as power below, but here one observation should be made. Particularly from the eighteenth century on, a distinctive feature of the mythos of modernity is the idea that we live in a uniquely scientific age where our knowledge has progressed way beyond primitive and superstitious attempts to understand the world. We know that our knowledge is true and their knowledge was false, because our knowledge *works* and gives us power over them. We could not have simply "discovered" and then "claimed" Australia (where I live) for the English Crown if we did not see ourselves as having "superior" power born of our "advanced" knowledge and technology, to wrest it from its original custodians by force.

Three characteristics of the collective human activity of modern knowledge is its affirmation of *reductive objectivity*, its tacit *individualism*, and its equation of validity with *instrumental power*. This is how we are formed to understand knowledge within modernity. Of course, postmodern thinkers often seek to reject this outlook[6] and typically embrace a form of radical relativism,

---

5. Bacon, *New Atlantis*.

6. I do not think that secular postmodernism escapes being modern. Assumptions of metaphysical univocity and materialism that are profoundly modern render the possibility of meaning itself untenable, which postmodern theorists like Lyotard and Derrida seem to understand, but modern positivists, rationalists, and pragmatists do not see. The postmodern critique of modern knowledge should be taken very seriously, but it is a critique from *within* the metaphysical and theological assumptions of modernity, and so it fails to be

which modernists find tantamount to being immorally post-truth. On modernism's side, facts *do* have some objective substance to them and interpretations are not endlessly plastic if meaning is to be treated as in any way communicable. And yet, both modernity and postmodernism are embedded in collective frames of worship that the Christian should in no manner blindly accept.

The doxological core of modern knowledge is what I will call the Principality of Man. This ruling principle is a collectively assumed species of epistemic anthropocentrism defined by autonomy, instrumental power, and a reductive filtering out of the non-quantifiable, the essentially meaningful, and the transcendent grounds of the immanent. This knowledge is a key feature of the doxological landscape of secular modernity.

Without acknowledging what it is that we are doing, we are self-worshipping idolaters, and knowledge is the altar on which we bow down to the powers of "man" in our times. Via modern knowledge we isolate ourselves from God and presume to rule the world, defining God in our own image as a maker and user of things in service of his own sovereign will. Unsurprisingly, when the real object of our highest loyalty is mastery of the world in the service of our own unbounded freedom of will, we find we do not need God. But when knowledge is merely instrumental its meaning evaporates and our freedom becomes a blind slavery to mere material necessity. It's a Tower of Babel thing. Fragmentation, oppression, and disintegration follow on from hubris, self-worship, and the aspiration for god-like power.

How can we live differently as citizens of the City of God?

If knowledge is a collective human activity, then the knowledge of the Christian needs to be informed by the formation context of the Christian community. I am not primarily speaking about sending our kids to Christian schools so that they learn the doctrines of the church within their schooling context as well as on Sundays. What I am speaking of is that knowledge itself must be understood differently within the practices and assumptions of

---

genuinely *post*modern, but is rather the natural self-defeating consequence of modern metaphysics and theology.

the Christian community from how it is now understood within secular modernity.

Knowledge is love. This is the Christian vision. Knowledge is a love grounded in a foundational relationship between each knower and God, and between all creatures within God's creation. This is so because God is love and has made the cosmos in love, and the love of Christ in the Passion reconciles us to God, to our neighbor, and to creation. The self-concerned refusal of this love is the refusal of the life of God given to us in love. The knowledge of love embedded in the life of Christ is not a knowledge of mastery, autonomous freedom, and unrestrained power functionally discrete from the realm of personal conviction.

It is our reductive and instrumental knowledge that gives power, and it is our Western technological power that is destroying the fecundity of the earth. Certainly, technology can be used for good or ill, but it is the supposed neutrality and disinterest of knowledge itself that ensures that our technologies are used for ill (i.e., the mere self-interest or convenience of the powerful). Love is not neutral and it is not disinterested. Love is interested in the flourishing and wellbeing of the other. Can we teach knowledge as interested and other-concerned in our day and age? Love is intrinsically value- and meaning-seeing. Can we think of knowledge in intrinsically value- and meaning-defined categories any more?

Increasingly our knowledge-institutions are instrumentally driven. Universities are now, at bottom line, all about money. Perhaps only Christian-based knowledge-institutions can resist this trend within secular modernity. Perhaps only Christian-based knowledge-institutions can think of knowledge as a function of love and right worship. If the church does not step into the knowledge arena the fragmentation and instrumentalization of knowledge will radically reshape our universities so as to make their original teleology unrecognizable. The point of learning is being lost, the doxologically situated value of truth is being lost, and the formation of the minds of our children and young adults is being directed towards merely instrumental goals in ways that are destructive of their humanity. If the church is not salt in this context, then our civilization can only go off; and if the church is not light in this context then our culture can only grow darker.

2. KNOWLEDGE IS ALWAYS EMBEDDED IN LANGUAGE

The intimate connection between language and meaningful thought is something one of Kierkegaard's few heroes—Johann Georg Hamann—understood very deeply.[7] Unsurprisingly, our understanding of what language is deeply shapes our view of what knowledge is.

To Hamann, all human language is a partial participation of created souls in the Logos of God, the true Meaning, Reason, and Source of creation. But to modernity, there is no divine mystery to meaning and reason, and there is no divine source to the mystery of being. Hence—after Spenser's agnostic Darwinism evolves into Russell's positivistic atheism—language within the mainstream of secular philosophy and the social sciences has its origin in the pragmatic communication of survival-enhancing facts. Language is simply a natural thing that has no innate connection with transcendence. Language has become to us meaning-neutral information, a tool for marketing and image-projection (and self-creation), and a means of instrumental power in a social context.

Doxologically, thinking of language as a purely human construct facilitates the "Principality of Man" in our knowledge-culture. Here Meaning itself—the Divine Logos—is not an objective reality that our knowledge partially and creatively comprehends, rather, meaning is a tool of anthropocentrically defined instrumental power. We largely assume that *we* are the source and locus of logos. This starts as a determined indifference to the possibility of meanings existing outside of materially defined interests, but ends as the reduction of knowledge to information and the reduction of public speech to a rigid procedural template that has no connection with substantive values or transcendent horizons. Here speech itself becomes subhuman.

7. Smith, *J. G. Hamann.*

In the mass-media age, the relentless propagation of what Kierkegaard describes as meaningless announcements (what we now call news) is a thick stream of banal information that claims helpful factual neutrality, but is never so. As Ellul points out,[8] the news was really the most excellent tool of public mind-management the technological society could produce before the rise of Facebook and Twitter. As Virilio points out, the production of collective fears via the mass media is one of the most powerful tools of controlling the herd spirits of the public.[9]

How then do we think about language as sociological theologians?

Firstly, we need to be aware that speech—all speech—is an astonishing spiritually participatory act. This is why blessings and cursings really mean something in the Bible. The words we speak and the knowledge we convey with those words is always, as James 3:6–12 puts it, a life-giving stream or a destructive fire from hell. Meaningful communication is never spiritually neutral. Just as Jesus, as a pious Jew, avoided the very touch of Roman money because it had the graven and idolatrous image of Caesar on it (Matt 22:15–22), so we would do well to avoid words that are defined by a merely instrumental conception of language. There are myriads of de-humanizing, instrumentalizing, amoralizing, de-transcendentalizing ways of speaking (and hence, acting) that the City of God should not blindly take up. For example, the discourses and practices that surround human resource management, national interest, marketing and promotions, entertainment, and social media define much of the social reality in which we live. And the dehumanization of those globally marginalized and displaced people deemed a threat to our own safe first-world standard of living (defined in purely material terms) are often portrayed to us via our own power projections and instrumental agendas that curse the image of God in the poor, the vulnerable, the non-competitive, and the alien in our (global) midst. Ways of speaking and ways of acting are mutually re-enforcing. It is no easy matter that the

---

8. See Ellul, *Propaganda*.

9. See Virilio, *The Administration of Fear*.

words of our mouths and the meditations of our heart will be acceptable in God's sight, for not only must our words and hearts be right, but their being right will result in the actions God requires (Jas 1:22).

This is all a bit sermonic—though it is true nonetheless—but sociologically the point is that as members of a community of speakers, the language of the gospel should be defining the syntax and semantics of our way of living as the City of God on pilgrimage. Conversely, the syntax and semantics of the City of Man is a very powerful force defining the public and private arenas of normal life within secular modernity, and this language has a doxological teleology directing our way of speaking and acting towards the worship of humanity. Kierkegaard powerfully outlines the way in which language sociologically shapes the City of Man in the garrulous and competitive norms of idolatrous self-manufacture as facilitated by the mass media native to the Present Age's comfortable urban life. We too, should notice this, and not let this language be the unobserved wallpaper to our lives, defining our outlook, speech, and actions in conformity to the City of Man, however religious we might be on a Sunday.[10]

3. KNOWLEDGE IS ALWAYS METAPHYSICALLY ENTANGLED

What we take to be real defines the way we categorize the difference between knowledge and fantasy, between sensible normal behavior and madness. Since the seventeenth century Western European understandings of reality have been defined by reductive understandings of mathematical reason and the empirical observation of physical appearances. But sociologically, metaphysics is not simply—not even primarily—a set of intellectual doctrines, rather it is a common assumed outlook on what really matters as

10. Public intellectuals who watch and evaluate the use and abuse of language are, to the theological sociologist, very important. For a fine example of this sort of work see, from Australia, Watson, *Gobbledegook*; from the US, Frankfurt, *On Bullshit*.

real.[11] So what interests us here is not simply what intellectual doctrines any given culture assumes when its people pursue and apply a valid knowledge of reality, but the relationship between assumed shared intellectual doctrines and assumed shared ways of knowing and living.

Let us start with the intellectual doctrines.

The reality beliefs that define our conception of a valid knowledge of reality predate but deeply shape the broad topography of the modern, secular, scientific worldview (and hence the modern, secular, scientific, sociological life-world in which we live and act). Here is a quick spin through the relevant terrain.

In the seventeenth century, the scholastic Christian Aristotelian understanding of reality collapsed. This collapse had something to do with Galileo and Copernicus, but actually, by the 1630s this older outlook had been under considerable stress for some centuries. The typical story we tend to believe is that when the evidence became irrefutable that the geo-centric cosmology endorsed by the Roman Catholic Church was simply wrong, then modern science was born and the medieval age of theologically distorted, factually wrong, and magically backward superstition came to an end. Actually, what happened bears little resemblance to this story.

In the history of Western ideas, since classical Greek times there have been three major families of ideas about the nature of reality (metaphysics). The first of these is Platonist. Here matter and form are what all tangible things are made of, but form itself is not material—it is intellective. Here the intellective (what we might now call the spiritual) is more foundational than the material, because the material is temporal and transient, but at least some ideas are eternal and unchanging. The high forms (ideas) native to this outlook—the *transcendentalia* of this vision of reality—are the eternal forms of the Good, the True, and the Beautiful, Being, and Unity. All of created reality participates in these divinely given high realities. All the transcendentals are integral with each other—i.e., the Good is always True and Beautiful, etc.—and yet there are different spheres of contemplation in relation to the

11. See Berger and Luckmann, *The Social Construction of Reality*.

transcendentalia. In terms of knowledge, those who contemplate justice and theology are seeking some knowledge of the Good; those who study what we would now call science and mathematics are seeking some knowledge of the True; those who practice and appreciate the arts are seeking the Beautiful. The Good is a special case here, because to Plato the Good is not only an eternal form, but it is the source of reality itself. Knowledge here is also love. Because the Real is a function of the Good, there can be no true knowledge of evil and no true knowledge that is not also spiritually transformative of the knower. So eternal forms are expressed partially in space and time, as are the lesser forms of all particular existing beings, and the cosmos is saturated with the divine Logos that expresses thought and meaning through (but not finally in) all phenomena. Significantly, the basic categories of this reality-vision are qualitative, intellective, and theological.

Platonist visions of the real come in a variety of flavors, but in one form or another (including patristic Christian forms) Platonist metaphysics dominated the classical world and Western culture from about the middle of the second century BC to the thirteenth century AD. This intrinsically theological outlook was replaced by a more scientific outlook that was still embedded in many of the theological premises of Platonist metaphysics in the late thirteenth century. This new metaphysical perspective is Aristotelian.

Aristotelian metaphysics—and as a distinct metaphysics, the only type of Aristotelianism that has become assumed in the West is Christian scholastic Aristotelianism—gives matter a much more prominent place in the matter/form matrix than Platonism did. Unlike for Aristotle himself, to the medievals the form of the human soul did survive the destruction of the matter of the human body, so scholastic Aristotelianism is considerably influenced by the metaphysics of Christian Platonism. And yet, we are moving from an essentially theological vision of the immaterial grounds of reality to a view where matter really matters. The deep interest in natural philosophy (what we would now call science) in Aristotle took off in the High Middle Ages.[12] The intricate science of

12. See Rubenstein, *Aristotle's Children*.

politics and ethics in combination with exacting Aristotelian logic flourished in the High Middle Ages. Aristotle is very this-world focused. But again, theological underpinnings, essential meanings, intrinsic purposes, and high spiritual realities define this scholastic vision of the real. The basic assumptions of Aristotelian metaphysics were largely assumed in Western culture from the thirteenth to the seventeenth centuries.

The third type of metaphysics that has defined the Western life-form actually predates both Plato and Aristotle in its origins, but does not take up a widespread and assumed hold of Western culture until the seventeenth century AD. This is Democritus' atomism. Here the stuff of reality is only matter, motion, and void (with no intellective essence, innate purpose, intrinsic value, or transcendent reality).

The profound shift away from both Platonist and Aristotelian metaphysical assumptions and to the Democritan corpuscular metaphysics of the seventeenth century is a very complex story with roots in the fourteenth century. Robert Pasnau details the intellectual complexities of the passage from medieval to early modern philosophy and Brad Gregory, aware of the intellectual issues, follows that same evolution, but with more emphasis on the religious and political dynamics of this shift.[13] Two intellectual features of this shift that make it such a far-reaching rupture from the Platonist and Aristotelian metaphysical roots of Western civilization are univocalism and ontological parsimony, which we shall briefly explore here.

Aquinas—from early in the scholastic Aristotelian revolution, yet still rooted in Augustine's Neoplatonist metaphysics—does not think reality itself is all that simple. That is, there are different orders of reality. The most fundamental order of reality—God—is beyond our normal categories of understanding and anything we say about who and what God is must be by means of analogy. The incarnation of God in Christ, and the revelation of God's interventions in human history are the most profound truths we can understand; but they are truths referring to a different order of

---

13. Pasnau, *Metaphysical Themes*; Gregory, *The Unintended Reformation*.

reality than the truths of what we would now call science. These first-order truths are not just of a different order of reality to science, but the world of science is dependent on this order of higher reality for both its material existence and intellective essences. This was taken as given in Aquinas' day, but it is not taken as given in our day. Yet, to Aquinas—in good Aristotelian fashion—nothing is grasped by our minds without being first apprehended by the senses. To Aquinas, this understanding of higher reality is itself only grasped by us—even though it is not a scientific category—through reflecting on our sensory experience of creation, the experiences of others recorded in history and the revelations of the church, and the experience of God in the mass and the community-life of the church, with the subtle aid of the Holy Spirit. So we understand the notion of reality from our experience of concrete real things that have an existence independent of our awareness of them, but we come to grasp that this notion of reality is not adequate to understand God, though it is the best analogy we have for understanding the Foundation and Source of reality, God. So to Aquinas, the notion of reality (being) is not univocal. That is, there is *more than one level of reality*, such that tangible reality is real, but the reality of God on which tangible reality depends— the really real—is only understandable to us by analogy. And, of course, the source of intellective essence—what it is that makes one being a particular entity of a certain species, and that which gives our minds the ability to grasp intellectual truths—is God. So reality is not univocal, but there are different layers to reality with the immediately perceived level being always dependent on the divine level that is not immediately apprehended by the senses. There is more than one sense to the word "real" to Aquinas.

However, Aquinas' conception of our analogical understanding of the being (reality) of God was contested very soon after Aquinas' time, for reasons we will not unpack here. But from the fourteenth century, the notion that reality (being) itself actually *is* univocal appears and starts to gain leverage on the Western mind. By the sixteenth century the idea of a sharp divide between a discrete realm of purely natural (and univocal) reality, and an equally discrete realm of the supernatural starts to isolate God from creation. This cuts off the ties between the being of God and the existence of creation that are basic to Aquinas' outlook. The fourteenth-century principle of ontological parsimony (commonly called Ockham's razor) also comes into play. This is the idea that if there is a simple explanation for anything, based only on logic and observation, then there is no need to posit the existence of any complex metaphysical entities that cannot be simply explained.

Other matters, such as the astonishing subtlety and inherent difficulty of the scholastic idea of prime matter, come into play, but essentially, Aristotelian metaphysics was staggeringly complex by the seventeenth century and forces seeking a univocal and parsimonious outlook on empirical and rational proof, and freedom from theological authorities, led to the collapse of Aristotelian metaphysics as soon as an alternative knowledge-system was available. When the modern scientific worldview was born—with Descartes and Galileo—and then solidified with Newton, it largely assumed a univocal and parsimonious metaphysics, with a conception of "pure nature" that was autonomous from any supernatural order of reality, and with no clear idea of essential form. Matter comprised of atoms, in motion, in void, was *all* that—for all practical and ordinary purposes—existed. And the enhancement of practical purposes was one of the original driving rationales of the new science. This type of metaphysics has been integral with modern knowledge from its very inception.

The point of the above very brief sketch of the three great ages of metaphysical thinking in Western intellectual history is fourfold. Firstly, we do not typically choose our basic culturally assumed conception of reality, but it is something we are *born into* and take for granted depending on where and when we are born. Within Western culture over the past two millennia there have been three very different sets of outlooks on reality, and these ways of seeing the world deeply shape how our communities have understood meaning, value, purpose, and realism. Secondly, none of these views of reality (as well as every other conceivable view on the nature of reality itself) are theologically neutral. Thirdly, because we often believe the myth of progress (because we know how to fly plains this means we are an advanced civilization in relation to all pre-scientific cultures), we tend to think of past metaphysical stances as superseded and backward, just because they are past. Fourthly, our prevailing view of reality is not compatible with an orthodox Christian understanding of creation. Let us explore this latter point a little.

Simon Oliver has written a very accessible book outlining how the assumptions of modern metaphysics make what I will call "modern theology" incompatible with a Christian understanding of both creation and God.[14] Because we tend to assume that reality is univocal, because our science is reductive and instrumental, we tend to create God in the image of our own univocal metaphysics and our own reductive and instrumental science. This makes God *a* being (not the grounds *of* being) and it makes God like us, only unlimited—a fabricator of things with total power and total freedom of will. That is, we construct God within the metaphysics and anthropology of modern "man"[15] (here is that Principality of Man again), and then either (idolatrously) worship that God, or reject that God as unprovable within the only categories of proof modernity will accept—reductively materialist and methodologically atheistic science. As David Bentley Hart points out, modern atheism is mistaken if it believes that the God it rejects ever was the God of serious Christian (or Hebrew or Islamic or Hindu) theology, so modern atheism is—ironically—actually aligned with

14. Oliver, *Creation*.

15. There is nothing distinctly modern about idolatry. Constructing the divine in our own image and then worshipping ourselves through deference to our gods is the main stay of ancient religion. The god Athena, for example, *is* the Athenians writ large and cast onto the cosmic stage, with all the powers and attributes that the Athenians wish to immortalize in the advancement of their own glory. Arguably, this is a basic pattern of religion, and it takes a very strong theology of the otherness of God to counter, to at least some extent, the deeply doxologically sinful drives embedded in religious practice and religious institutions.

a serious theology of God and creation in its very rejection of modernity's god.[16]

The shocking truth is that modern theology is incompatible with a Christian understanding of both God and creation, and the knowledge and metaphysics of modernity are—theologically—anti-Christian. That is, the metaphysical assumptions native to the New Testament, as upheld by both the Christian Platonist outlook of Augustine and the scholastic Aristotelian outlook of Aquinas, cannot be extracted from the Christian understanding of God and creation and still give you a Christian understanding of God and creation.[17] This means that the thought and practice world modern Christians are living within is a City of Man that does not comprehend a Christian understanding of God and creation. This is so, even though—ironically—the history of modernity and modern knowledge is driven forward by the theological developments that predate the Reformation. Western Christianity—both Roman Catholic and Protestant—birthed this modern approach to reality and knowledge.

If we wish to think doxologically about the sociology of knowledge within the context of the broadly modern secular Western life-world, we are faced with a very demanding challenge. The way we think of reality, know reality, and function realistically with others is almost inescapably prone to the idolatry of the City of Man. In some regards, this is to be expected if one is aware of the New Testament teaching about the kingdom of God and the world. On the other hand, it is often a deep shock to professing Christians to realize that it is *we* who have generated the underpinning metaphysical and epistemological assumptions of the world in our times.

16. Hart, *Experience of God.*
17. Tyson, *Returning to Reality.*

4. KNOWLEDGE IS NEVER THEOLOGICALLY OR POLITICALLY NEUTRAL

Let us look at the theological nature of knowledge.

As outlined above, if one interprets the meaning of the facts of nature from within the Christian doctrine of creation (and fall) one will understand the meaning of natural phenomena in a different way to if one does not have an orthodox theology of creation and social realities as fundamental as sin and redemption. That you can have different understandings of the meaning of human life does not mean that the observable facts of, for example, normal medical science are in dispute. But the way questions of policy are made that relate to the dignity of hospital patients and the meaning of health and death, for example, is always entangled in either good theology or bad theology (doxological frames of ultimate value and purpose) or the impossible attempt to have no theology.

Interestingly, there was no science-verses-religion war going on in the 1840s—that war was not invented until well after Kierkegaard died—so Kierkegaard had no interest in the kinds of science and religion issues that often define popular discourse in this area today. But Kierkegaard gave profound attention to the nature of true knowledge in his *Concluding Unscientific Postscript*. To Kierkegaard, sin and faith are the most basic categories of truth and falsehood in our actual existence. If it is true that God is our Creator, if it is true that we cannot escape the seriousness of our responsibility before eternity by an appeal to objective neutrality, then we must accept that knowledge *always* has a theological coloring of one sort or another.

The idea that knowledge has no theological color is an abstraction that is not knowledge as we actually know. Knowledge does not exist independently of knowers, and human knowers are always communally, morally, and doxologically situated beings. So the relation of the existing human being to the Source of being, to the origin and destiny of creation, within a community of interpretation and formation, is inherently entangled in all knowledge.

The cathedral schools that became the Western universities arose out of an appreciation of just this reality. The devotional contemplation of truth is the doxological act at the origin of our own intellectual tradition.

What does this mean sociologically?

Christians should expect to know the world in a manner informed by our theology, which is not compatible with the normal outlook assumed by the theological assumptions of secular modernity. Economics and politics are good cases in point.

Today political realism and neoliberal economic common sense are informed by a theological frame incompatible with an orthodox Christian understanding of the meaning of wealth and power, and by the doxological cores presupposed by political realism and neoliberal economics. Christians are often supporters of this situation for a number of reasons, one of which is that a distorted Christian theology actually underpins political realism and neoliberal economics. Christians should not simply accept this, however, but need to become sensitive theological readers of the knowledge discourses that are assumed by the life-world in which we live.

A Hobbesian understanding the inherent violence of human nature, a Machiavellian understanding of amoral public relations and cunning pragmatism in power (political realism), and Adam Smith's understanding of minimally regulated market forces driven by the engine of self-interest as the basis of good economic order deeply define our knowledge and practice concerning power[18] and money.[19] They are all secularized versions of post-fourteenth-century voluntarist theology (where the primary quality of God is sovereign *will*, and where human nature made in the image of God aspires to unfettered sovereign *power* over our own sphere of authority), presupposing a functionally univocal order of reality that is discrete from the supernatural interference of God, and they presuppose a secularized conception of the fall of man such that evil and amoral behavior coupled with social power, and

18. See Campolo, *The Power Delusion.*

19. See Brueggemann, *Money and Possessions.*

self-interested behavior coupled with private wealth, are entirely natural.

Out of this conception of God—and our being made in *that* image—arises an insatiable quest for total knowledge that is intimately tied up with instrumental mastery: power. I do not wish to claim that this understanding is unequivocally anti-Christian, for while all the conceptions of God we have are analogical and inadequate, nonetheless humility and Christ-following discipleship does enable right worship, even when our theology is seriously inadequate. But there really are theological problems with how knowledge, power, and mastery have played out in the West.

In Western modernity, science is related very directly to technology and technology to the means of mastery over both nature and others. Without the pragmatic superiority of military and naval technology the violent colonial mastery of the entire globe by European powers could not have happened. Globalization is a function of Western technology. Without Western-originated information technology our system of global financial markets would never have appeared. Without modern technology the man-made pending environmental crisis of the biosphere would not have been possible.[20] The idea that modern knowledge and the creation of technologies from that knowledge are somehow morally neutral is impossibly naïve.

Neither is such power theologically neutral. It is a function of a hubristic push to create ourselves in the image of the voluntarist, fabricating God worshipped—in action if not in religion—by the pioneering discoverers, inventors, and merchants of modern Europe. There are other models of knowledge that are not so inherently voluntaristic, anthropocentric, and instrumental. Notably, indigenous epistemologies that adapt the human to the natural and spiritually alive existing order are, at least in that regard,

20. For a few important books on the rate of man-made environmental change, and the politics, commercial interest, and theology surrounding this, see McNeil and Engelke, *The Great Acceleration*; Hamilton, *The Anthropocene and the Global Environmental Crisis*; Oreskes and Conway, *Merchants of Doubt*; Serreze, *Brave New Arctic*; Northcott, *A Political Theology of Climate Change*.

84

astonishingly theologically superior to Western epistemology.[21] But we moderns have now almost wiped those ways of knowing— as functional sociological life-forms—out.

KIERKEGAARD'S DOXOLOGICAL SOCIOLOGY AND KNOWLEDGE

Kierkegaard maintains that only if each individual grounds themselves adequately in the exclusive primal relationship that is fundamental for them to be a self—the ontologically dependent relationship between the creature and the Creator—can true sociality (social relations grounded in truth) result. If something is inadequate in the way an individual rests in that power that establishes the self (God), this failure of primal existential good faith produces an insatiable doxological lack in the individual that is manifest in sinful social relations that vainly seek to substitute gods of our own making for God and selves of our own making for real individuals. Thus, doxology is the basic origin of social life-forms; forms either aspiring towards good faith in the love of God and neighbor, or idolatrous life-forms producing all the usual social and psychological pathologies of the vain love of self. Kierkegaard is thus profoundly Augustinian (as every good Lutheran should be).

Thinking about knowledge in this context is fascinating. The culturally assumed modern secular configuration of knowledge has no conception of its doxological loading, being under the misapprehension that knowledge is objective and rational in a manner independent of something as subjective as theology or as optional as worship. That is, from Kierkegaard's perspective, modern knowledge is a hopeless abstraction facilitating a blindness to

---

21. Of course, the pagan worship of spiritually understood natural powers is idolatrous to Christian theology. Yet, the recognition of a pre-established divinely ordained and upheld natural order and the humility to find our place in that order is implied in the charge of rulership given to Adam in his sinless state (this is a *stewardship* rather than a use-and-abuse conception of total voluntarist sovereignty).

our real doxological situation as existing knowers. But this blindness is not just a privation of insight, it is the basic engine of sin in our epistemic frameworks and in the structures of power, action, and inter-relation premised on that collective framework. Knowledge is not, and cannot be, doxologically neutral, other than in an existentially trivial sense. That we only think of knowledge in existentially trivial terms is the great anti-theological triumph of our life-world. But this is not a triumph that the Christian can mildly accept. And its triumph makes our knowledge of social relations and psychological dynamics inherently misguided, regardless of the empirical rigor and conceptual sophistication of the vast structures of existentially trivial knowledge about the soul and society that we do now have. This epistemic sin—the failure to hit the mark of meaningful knowledge—facilitates stunning pathologies in our use and understanding of power.

This chapter has been pretty theoretically heavy. Let us now turn from the idolatrous tendencies of the epistemic and metaphysical signatures of modern knowledge to a couple of very concrete features of our daily lives: money and religion.

7

Money

WHAT IS MONEY?

SOCIOLOGICALLY, FEW THINGS ARE more fascinating than money. Money is pretty well a pure social construct, for it has no existence outside of the context of human societies. Coins, bank notes, and electronically stored numbers in a bank account have no value or meaning (and, in the case of a bank account, almost no physical reality) outside of the use those token objects/cyphers have as a means of exchange and power in our societies. So the first thing we need to do in thinking sociologically about money is drop the essential social fiction that makes money work; the fiction that money has an objective reality in its own right.

You can't eat money, you can't build a house with it, and while the graven images on coins may be beautiful objects of craftsmanship, there is no aesthetic value in money itself as there is, say, in art. And yet because we are given money for our labor, and because others will give us real objects of need and value in exchange for money, the task of acquiring money dominates most of our lives in one way or another. In sociological terms, money is a foundational feature of the social realities we inhabit, so it is in that sense very,

very real. And yet it is nothing in itself and it has no reality as a valid means of exchange unless we all believe in and—in good faith—act upon that constructed validity. Common social values and collective practices give money its value, its use, its power, and its (very strange) reality.

In many ways—at least for the rich—money is a wonderful invention. And yet, for the majority of people who have lived in societies where money governs exchange, most people have struggled to acquire enough money to be comfortable and secure. It seems that moneyed societies more or less naturally develop minority elites who are rich and powerful, and who ensure the perpetuation of their elite position by means of being rich and powerful in comparison with the majority. In the normal course of things it takes money to make money, which means that even if you work hard and have enough money for your needs, unless you can save or invest some surplus money, you will always be living from hand to mouth.

Societies are stratified and money is a means of perpetuating power and privilege stratification in societies. Money itself is not anything, but as the means of governing exchange in societies, money gains a life of its own. This points to a significant paradox in the nature of money. Money has no real existence in its own right, and is a pure social construct. This should mean that we can govern and structure money however we like. In (social) reality, though, money takes on a life of its own and becomes a governing principle within the societies that construct and use it.

MONEY AND DOXOLOGY

Jesus famously said "No one can serve two masters. Either you will hate one and love the other, or you will be devoted to the one and despise the other. You cannot serve both God and Money" (Matt 6:24). We are born into and embedded in societies and—being creatures that are innately doxological beings—this means that the structures of our society are integral with the final objects of value and authority upheld as normative within our society. The

Jews in first-century Palestine sought to integrate the role of labor and wealth accumulation within their society to a place that was subservient to the origin and source of value—God. However, the rise of mammon above God is an ever-present risk in societies for, as noted above, money takes on a reality of its own that is intimately enmeshed in our daily lives of labor and exchange, and in the structures that stratify power and privilege. The message of Christ seems clear; unless you make a concerted attempt to keep the power of money subservient to God as the locus and source of true value, you will make God functionally subservient to mammon.

In the Hebraic context in which Jesus lived, a significant practice of subordinating the practices of labor and exchange to God was Sabbath observance. Fascinatingly, Jesus is often taken to task by the powerful and respected elites of his own community on the grounds of infringing the Sabbath. This points to the natural alliance between religion and power such that the worship of God is—in pre-secular societies—a very palpable means of perpetuating social controls. Jesus calls his critics out on their doxological integrity asserting that they are hypocritically pedantic about Sabbath observance when, should serious economic loss be a possibility, Sabbath observance can be overridden (Matt 12:11). But the matter is complex, for Jesus also asserts that Sabbath observance should not be absolutized as if humanity was made for the Sabbath (Mark 2:27) and as if normal human values must be held subordinate to pedantic religious observance (Luke 14:5).

So how are we to think about money and worship today?

MONEY AND WORSHIP

Our liberal, secular, and materially focused life-world has constructed a discretely private realm for religion and spirituality that is at least notionally locked off from the public world of commerce and financial power. Yet actually, commerce and finance are much more religious than we like to admit. For our public sphere is deeply shaped by the value system (a system of relative worth—a worth-ship hierarchy) of market-driven, financialized, entrepreneurial, and speculative capitalism. Indeed, our politicians and public institutions now largely take it as given that the innovative pursuit of personal wealth is the highest common good of our shared public way of life. This is because we are committed to secular liberalism. "Secular" here means we uphold the separation of church from state such that the church only has authority in private spiritual matters. "Liberal" here means we reject the idea that there is any divinely mandated authority that can set before us a frame of values and meanings that define the true common good. No, to us, each individual is alone the judge of ultimate value and meaning. Everyone is more or less required to build their own worth-orienting idol, even if we are seeking to worship the one true God.[1] Because no public common good can be qualitatively and doxologically defined, the functional public common good becomes the pursuit of each person's private goods. Yet because money and commerce is actually a public and interpersonal concern, there must actually be common governing values and norms in our commerce and finance. In this context, mere negative individual freedom (freedom from authoritative qualitative and worship orthodoxy) and a discourse that elides all questions of ultimate meaning (and intrinsic meaning) *becomes* the highest good—the first object of collective worth. Put differently, because the qualitative and the transcendent is officially outside of the public realm, only the quantitative and the material *can* define the public common good. Here, mammon—the quantitative accumulation of financial power as the highest end of public life—is the obvious candidate to be the doxological core of consumer culture.

Functionally, modern, liberal, capitalist societies have no inbuilt religious protections against the pursuit of monetary accumulation (mammon) becoming the first and collectively unifying object of corporate worship.[2] What this means is that we are

---

1. That is, where religion is thought of as a discretely personal and private freedom, my belief in the one true God is treated as my personal object of worth (my household idol) in the public arena.

2. Of course, the fabulous wealth of the medieval papacy generated all

naturally formed by our environment to be functional devotees of mammon, without even knowing it.

Scholars looking at mammon and the place of money and possessions in the scriptures point out that things from within the Jewish and Christian traditions are on the one hand doxologically black and white, and on the other hand practically grey.[3] The commands of God are clear: the love and worship of God, and the love of neighbor must come before the pursuit of monetary accumulation. Further, graven images of Caesar as a divinity on Roman coins were doxologically problematic for Jews. Yet practically, the Roman coin was necessary for trade and tax. Thus, the threat of idolatry was ever present at the same time that the money and trading systems of the gentile and idolatrous Roman Imperium were unavoidable. This was an inherently edgy dynamic. But for us, we hardly think of the pursuit of financial accumulation as doxological, and we tend to assume that if we pay our tax and don't lie or steal, then one can be a good Christian at the same time as making monetary accumulation the first priority of our professional time and energy.

But how should we think—doxologically—about the incredible power that mammon has over the life-world *we* inhabit?

We live in workplace contexts where increasingly the bottom line of all the purposes and operational norms of the organizations that employ us is . . . the bottom line. That is, employees and institutional purposes are subordinate to monetary viability. We even think of working people as "human resources"—as things that are raw material for the use of the institution in fulfilling its first purpose—making money.

In any secular business or government service, God, of course, is safely cordoned off from the goals and norms of the

---

manner of moral and political pathologies within the power center of the Roman church, and notions like "just price" embedded what modern economic thinkers would describe as structural market inefficiencies into medieval economics, and yet economic theory in the Middle Ages was integrated with doxological and moral concerns in a manner now inconceivable to neoliberal economic theorists.

3. See, Ellul, *Money and Power*; Brueggemann, *Money and Possessions*.

corporate entity, and placed firmly in the discretely private sphere of personal religious conviction. This is the doxological dynamic of pride. We are not creatures entrusted with stewardship over the resources of the earth by our Creator, we are not charged with responsibility for the care and flourishing of our neighbor—the two great doxologically orienting commandments have no contact with realistic and sound business management. We now believe a secularized Thomas Hobbes and Adam Smith over the Torah.[4] So the making of money becomes a discretely secular affair cordoned off from what is actually most central to our humanity—the love of God and the love of neighbor.

In religious organizations—churches—and institutions with explicitly humanitarian purposes—hospitals, schools, universities, charities, etc.—the bottom line is still the bottom line. Increasingly the logic of secular business management, marketing, human re-sources, fiscal health, and econometric pragmatism have the final say on what can and cannot be done and on how things are done. The functional purpose of financial viability becomes, in practice, the final purpose of the organization.

In recent times this deep societal swing towards an institu-tional logic of mammon has a particular history. This history is worth briefly outlining because our problem is not sound business management, but the displacement of higher ends for mere finan-cial viability, and this displacement itself has doxological drivers.

---

4. Of course, Hobbes and Smith are complex and profound thinkers on politics and economics, so the above sentence is not meant to be anything oth-er than a passing comment. Yet Hobbes' notion that social arrangements are naturally violent, so total violence should be invested in the state, and Smith's notion that self-interest produces the best economic outcome for all, have in-creasingly been extracted from their original (if still problematic) moral and theological frameworks, such that the fall has now been naturalized and the love of God and the love of neighbor have been extracted from the political and economic realisms of our times.

A BRIEF HISTORY OF THE POST-WAR RISE OF MAMMON

The post-war boom from 1949 to 1971 was Western capitalism's golden age. Sustained low inflation, high employment, and economic growth characterized the non-communist, US-dominated first world during this period. In countries like Australia, manufacturing, agriculture, and primary resources were boom sectors, enormous public works programs in hydro-electricity and the like flourished, state-funded common goods—public hospitals, schools, and universities—were set up and liberally funded, and social services that facilitated a common minimum standard of dignity and care were available to all. This was a tide of work, wealth, and dignity that lifted (nearly) all boats. The post-war international financial order was set up at Bretton Woods in the closing months of World War II, and much of the stability and prosperity of the post-war boom can be attributed to that architecture and the enormous reconstructive generosity of the surplus economy of the USA. The US rebuilt Germany and Japan and set about enhancing its global military power in order to make sure that the USSR and China—its ideological rivals—did not threaten the democratic freedoms and "Christian" values it espoused. Well, it all came unstuck in the 1970s.

By the late 1960s, the US economy had swung from surplus to deficit due to the cost of the enormously expensive Cold War. The global currency of "the free world" was the US dollar, and the value of the dollar had been pegged to gold (the US had staggering reserves of gold in the early post-war years) at $35 US an ounce. When European users of the US dollar realized that the US was printing more money than they had gold to back, they pushed the US to exchange currency for gold. The French pushed hard, and President Nixon's response in 1971 was to simply drop the gold standard. The US dollar floated free and international chaos ensued, exacerbated by enormous price hikes in oil. The Bretton Woods system was now broken. The 1970s saw stagflation—rising unemployment and rising inflation—interest rates went wild, and the post-war boom was over. The "answer" to this chaos arrived in the 1980s with Regan and Thatcher: neoliberal economic ideology. Actually, that answer was produced by the Nixon administration in the 1970s, but it was only effectively politically sold to voting publics in the mid-1980s.

What Nixon had done was maintain the US global hegemony while swinging the US-controlled global economy from being driven by the *surplus* economy of the US to being driven by the *deficit* economy of the US.[5] The wild-west finance sector of un-regulated bulls and bears that had caused the Great Depression had been strongly disciplined in the Bretton Woods order—an order that Nixon ended in 1971. To keep the US on top, Nixon set about liberating the bulls and bears of Wall Street in order to suck global money back into the US through its financial casino, even though the US currency had become a fiat currency. Brushing over the cataclysmic upheavals of the 1970s (which US financial policy wonks clearly understood),[6] the strategy worked like a charm.

The end result of this titanic shift of gears in the global economic order was a move in power away from political economics—with its concerns about work, production, and the commonwealth of the nation—to international high finance. Stock market trading, currency trading, speculative financial instruments, pumped-up real estate bubbles, and the rise of the multi-national corporation and the international tax-haven-protected super rich, displaced political economics in the 1980s. This is *the financialization of power.*[7]

Ironically, financialization was sold to the democracies of "the free world" as an economic necessity required to fix the problems

---

5. Varoufakis, *The Global Minotaur*, 94–96, 26–89.

6. Paul Volker, Chairman of the US Federal Reserve in the late 1970s and most of the 1980s, had been appointed undersecretary of the US treasury for international monetary affairs by Nixon in 1970. In this capacity he had recommended to Nixon that the Bretton Woods system be abandoned to keep US global hegemony afloat. In 1978 he gave a speech at the University of Warwick where he explained that a "controlled disintegration in the world economy is a legitimate objective for the 1980s." Cited in Varoufakis, *Global Minotaur*, 100.

7. See Das, *Extreme Money.*

of the 1970s, problems that were blamed on the protecting of manufacturing sectors and government spending on the common wealth of the nation. To supposedly secure jobs, manufacturing protections were dropped. Unsurprisingly, manufacturing in most of the first world withered in the 1970s and died in the 1980s. Those who could not survive in the new global economy could not irresponsibly expect a cushy government-subsidized ride anymore; they would simply perish, and it was on their own head. Money needed to be free to go wherever it would get a good return—lucrative factories in Indonesia, etc.—and high-tech service sectors in the first world would replace the manufacturing sector that had gone off shore, and the agricultural sector that had been replaced by heavy farming machinery. Exploiting cheap off-shore labor and resources for all our manufactured goods and basic needs would liberate the lean and innovative entrepreneurs in creating new jobs and new wealth creation that were not even thought of in the post-war boom era. Going with globalizing neoliberal economic necessity would produce jobs and wealth for us all.[8] In the 1980s,

8. Why anyone ever believed this is hard to see. Indeed, many in the 1980s saw right through the neoliberal globalization political sales pitch. A few examples of clarity from Australia during that era are Clark, *A Short History of Australia*, 322–52; Pusey, *Economic Rationalism in Canberra*; Jaensch, *The Hawke-Keating Hijack*. For clearly, there are only so many elite high-tech jobs in any national economy, and this is not where most money in the post-1980s first world has come from anyway. What actually happened to employment from the 1980s on was a huge burgeoning in the insecure low-tech service sector (making coffee, cleaning, dog-walking, etc.) as manufacturing and agriculture collapsed as employment sectors. This shift from production to services also saw the general casualization of most sectors of the workforce (including highly skilled sectors such as academics) whilst the elites in the financial sector, law, management, advertising, and real estate flew off the top of the income-distribution scale. From the post-war boom, when rich and poor alike improved in their lot and the overall effect was a greater egalitarianism of common wealth, the post-1980s trend has been increased income inequality and what we now call the two-speed economy. Here the top gear of the economy is the high-flying (often international or internationally linked) elites and those who have benefitted from the huge inflation in real estate and shares (a roaring 20s phenomenon), and the bottom gear is the relentlessly insecure low-income class. The middle class is badly stressed with powerful pressures to seek to rise up into the elite or fall down into the underclass. Michael Pusey outlines

this was politically sold to us as both inevitable and exciting. And, like suckers, we bought it.

This macro shift in the global order—a shift in power from economics to finance—has come to influence everything about how we now work and live. Economics itself is not firstly concerned with money—it is concerned with production, with work, with the distribution of necessary goods and services, and political economics is concerned with how these matters relate to questions of justice and the common good. But finance is concerned only with the accumulation of money. Now a bank may perform a valuable human function if it is genuinely interested in the well-being of its customers, but there is nothing intrinsic to a bank that requires it to be concerned with something other than the accumulation of its own financial power. A bank does not make anything, it only loans out money (money it does not have—apart from one twentieth of its loaning power—until the debtor pays it back, with interest) and its success as a bank is only measured by how much money it has accumulated for itself in the process of lending and investing money. This is an institution inherently prone to the doxological idol of mammon.

But it is not that the finance sector is the *cause* of our doxological problems. Rather, if we are thinking like Kierkegaard, our doxological problems give rise to a collective value-orienting idol like financialization. The post-war boom era gave rise to a generation of young people who were so used to material wealth and the pursuit of personal pleasure that an egoistic doxological tendency was something of a birthright to this generation.

A DOXOLOGICAL SOCIOLOGY OF MAMMON

Mammon is a deeply entrenched doxological principle as a governing power in our life-world. The doxological principle that Christ refers to explicitly when discussing this matter is that once

---

these processes in Australia: see, Pusey, *The Experience of Middle Australia*. The neoliberal push has not produced jobs and prosperity for the common citizen of first-world countries at all.

one starts down this road, in the end one cannot ultimately serve any god other than mammon. Our institutions lose their telos in any intrinsic value, any higher meaning, and any ultimate frame of truth, beauty, and goodness, under the conditions of a pragmatic materialist financialization. We all become means to the accumulation of wealth when we work for institutions and within nations where the final doxological common center is mammon. This is a profoundly dehumanizing trajectory, and our society is going down this trajectory at a rate of knots because we will not stop to ask, are we worshiping a false god?

Here is an opportunity for Christians to live differently as a witness to true worship. If in our own lives and the lives of Christian institutions, money can be a means to doing valuable things, and if merely monetized measures do not set the terms in how we evaluate the worth of workers and their work—this is moving contrary to the doxological trends of our age. Christians may well end up as workplace martyrs in an age were success in one's career and wealth are largely embedded within the necessities and worship of mammon. Many people are discarded in this game of elite high-flying winners and the mass of low-paid losers. Christians should be with the outcasts and uphold their dignity rather than embracing the agonistic moralism of mammon.

But let us get more concrete. Let us think about religion.

8

Religion

WHAT IS RELIGION?

SCHOLARS IN THE MODERN study of religion arena have found "religion" notoriously hard to define. When you try and locate what the common religious features are of ancient Australian Aboriginal life, contemporary Hindus, and modern Southern Baptists, the problem becomes unsolvable.[1] Perhaps there is a simple reason for this: we are looking for something that does not exist. Wilfred Cantwell Smith seems to have argued along these lines when he pointed out that our modern Western conception of religion is a distinct and new social organization that cannot be mapped onto non-modern and non-Western people at all.[2] That is, a modern understanding of what discretely religious beliefs and practices are

1. The problem is not just between these three categories but within them. There are many hundreds of distinct language and kinship nations across the Australian continent, each with an ancient lineage; in reality there is no such thing as a single unified Hindu religion; even Southern Baptists are far from homogeneous in doctrine and practice.

2. Smith, *The Meaning and End of Religion*, 18–19. See also Harrison, *The Territories of Science and Religion*, 7–11.

is not meaningfully applicable to even medieval Europe, let alone classical antiquity or non-Western people, and whether it means a lot even within Western modernity is hard to say.

In this chapter I am not interested in a modern understanding of what counts as a discretely religious belief or practice. I am not looking for discretely religious beliefs and practices that can be separated out from mundane, instrumental, and non-ritual practices and beliefs. Rather, I am interested in religion as the doxological glue that holds *all* human communities—be they deemed scared or secular—together, in whatever they are doing. If Kierkegaard is right, all individuals are doxological beings, thus all communities require doxologically shaped norms, whether people are—in a modern sense—religious or not. Dropping a modern understanding of religion, the definition of religion that I will work with in this chapter harks back to Augustine's understanding of the Latin word *religare*,[3] from which we get the English word "ligament," meaning the connective tissue that bind together the parts of a body.[4]

In Augustine's classical context, as William Cavanaugh notes, *religio* was not so much about discrete supernatural beliefs, as about practice, and practice that concerns *all* aspects of life: mundane, commercial, familial, and public. Clearly, in classical Rome, religion was not separate from the political, as "*religio* was inextricable from duty to the emperor and to the gods of Roman civic life."[5] Here the worship of God/gods, loyalty to one's political community, and piety and appropriateness in one's filial, civic, neighborly, and commercial relations, could not in any meaning-

3. Augustine, *City of God*, X, i. Augustine, *Of True Religion*.

4. Interestingly, *re-ligio* seems to recognize cultus and upholding all manner of social norms as a sort of remedial venture that seeks to unify a communal body, and a human-to-divine relation, that is found in a sundered state from the outset. Religion, like ethics, seems itself to be indicative that something is wrong from the start in human society. Just as Bonhoeffer (*Ethics*) argues that the very notion of Christian ethics signals a fall, so the very notion of cultus signals a fall. To Christian theology, there will be no ethics and no religion in the eschaton.

5. Cavanaugh, *The Myth of Religious Violence*, 61.

ful way be separated out. Indeed, performing the right actions, regardless of whether one had any "religious" beliefs concerning deities, was all that mattered here. To not sprinkle incense on an altar to the emperor was a seditious action, whether or not one actually believed the emperor was divine. Religion in its classical context is about the manner in which communities are bound together and the manner in which the common actions of worship are integral to the coherence and functionality of the common life of any community.

Augustine's outlook provides us with a very helpful way of understanding religion sociologically. Certainly Durkheim went some way toward this outlook in endeavoring to isolate the realm of individual active freedom (the secular) from the realm of public symbolic conformity (the sacred).[6] What is inadequate about Durkheim's understanding of the deep archetypes out of which modern society develops is not his understanding that the religious is what defines meaningful community unification, but his reductive sense that the religious ritual is simply (that is, non-spiritually, non-metaphysically) the communal. To Durkheim, modern society has outgrown a religious consciousness, which has bequeathed to it the problems of anomia and the fragmentation and disintegration of the very possibility of communal meaning. I am sure Durkheim has many powerful insights here, but we should not forget that the modern secular realm of individual freedom is defined *as a sacral public good*, and hence remains essentially religiously situated in post-Christian individual-freedom-focused societies.

Let us briefly explore how what we think of as "secular" categories are actually better understood as religious features of our way of life.[7]

---

6. Durkheim, *The Elementary Forms of the Religious Life.*

7. Two excellent texts on this concern are Asad, *Formations of the Secular* and Asad, *Genealogies of Religion.*

RELIGION IS THE DOXOLOGICAL
SOCIAL UNIFIER

I am an Australian. I recently visited the United States of America for the first time. I was amazed by the ubiquity and depth of the civic cult I saw. The American flag was omnipresent—on banks, on houses, on schools, on shops, in churches. Reverence for US military personal was manifest in prominent public shrines to huge numbers of war dead, and re-enforced at airports, where military personnel get on the plane first. "God bless America" was a common phrase in public announcements mentioning the military. I walked past a public rally in Central Park New York which was being opened by an operatic sounding woman singing the American national anthem. All those watching on stood respectfully with their hats off and their hands over their hearts (I understand this happens at football games too) whilst the sacred strains of the star-spangled banner were being belted out with high emotional octane.

This is secular worship. This is a sacralizing ritual around the nation state that unifies an otherwise deeply class- and race-divided and highly competitive conglomerate of individuals. American public worship—even in post-Christian, libertarian, secular New York—is strongly *religious* in its nature. There is a unifying doxological focus here that enables American civic life to exist. For there is no body without ligaments. And there is no unity to a body's actions without a head. Civic life is not possible without communally binding rituals, norms, and practices that are directed in their common intentions and commitments by some unifying and ordering principle, towards some collective end.

I am not seeking to argue that nationalism, or even imperialism, is inherently idolatrous. However, what unifies people and defines norms is always inherently *doxological* (oriented to a frame of worth) such that the risk of idolatry is always present in any doxological context. If there is nothing higher than the flag in the common public life of a people, then the nation is that public's idol. If there is nothing higher than the pursuit of money in the common commercial life of a people, then mammon has displaced the love of God, and money is the idol of their commercial community. If the enormous resources of the advertising industry are exerted to form us to be consumers such that the market is the first principle that consumer society serves, then the market is the god of consumer society. If this is the case, then the secular nation, the secular financial system, and the secular market are all inherently *religious*, whether or not we who participate in these common modes of life have any discretely religious convictions and practices.

With this in mind, let us think about what a few of the worship centers of our way of life are, how those centers are prone to idolatry, and how Christians might engage those centers redemptively. Three sites of modern religion that we will briefly touch on are sport, shopping, and technology. The categories of analysis that we can draw from these doxological activities can be applied to any other area of our way of life as well. We will use Kierkegaard's doxological sociology analytically, and Augustine's advice on how to counter idolatry proscriptively: "love, and then do as you will."[8]

SPORT

Kierkegaard's sociological key tells us that when individuals disregard their first doxological priority to love God, then they will vainly look for themselves in false objects of worship that are, in the final analysis, idols. Social structures will then be set up and developed that normalize and facilitate the vanity and idolatry of false worship, which the idolatrous community requires. Let us think about how this plays out in a very significant feature of mass-media facilitated public life—professional sport.

Let us draw on Augustine to think theologically about what a public spectacle is to start with.

8. Augustine, *7th homily on 1 John*, in Schaff, *Nicene and Post-Nicene Fathers*, Vol. VII, 504.

The spectacle culture of the Roman arena was—as Chanon Ross points out—explicitly set up to be doxological.[9] Daemons—intermediary divine beings, situated above people in that they are immortal, but beneath God, in that they have the same passions and desires that we have—were fully integral with the arena spectacle. Pompa—processions from a god's (daemon's) temple to the arena—signaled the start of the blood sacrifices to power and the mob.

In the arena the crowd was physically elevated and metaphysically positioned to a place above the life-and-death struggles on the arena floor. Being unlike those dying in the mortal realm, the thrill of spilt blood was a participatory sacrament facilitating vicarious daemonic elevation in the crowd. The crowd demanded blood. The crowd occupied the position of the daemons, between mortals and the high divine. On the arena floor great acts of prowess, violence, tragedy, and courage were being played out by high-end gladiators in defiance of the mortality of the human lot; glory in death was the only way for mortal man to defy the heartless fates that governed the affairs of men.[10] So both the crowd, as passive spectators, and the gladiators, as active participants in death-defying heroism, participated in the daemonic in the arena games of ancient Rome. The whole process was deeply tangled up with the glory of the Roman imperium itself and facilitated by the financial power of the political elites who used the daemonic satisfactions of the masses for their own advancement in populist power.

Augustine astutely notices two things here. Firstly, should someone seek to move from the daemonically satiated formation context of the Roman crowd to become a citizen of the City of God, they would need deliverance. Deliverance was an important aspect of the long and serious process of early church catechesis before baptism. Secondly, the first object of idolatry in the City

---

9. Ross, *Gift Glittering and Poisoned*, 55–59.

10. The gladiators were in this regard unlike the *noxii*, low-level criminals who were fed to wild beasts or brutally tortured and slaughtered simply to satisfy the bloodlust of the crowd.

of Man is always self-love. Disordered love is at the heart of all individual and collectively framed idolatry. So self-love was the doxological core of the spectacle, and being possessed by the powers of the arena spectacle entailed aspirations to a false divinity and vicarious self-aggrandizement through the heroes and the empire that the spectacle provided.

On the one hand, I am tempted to say nothing much has changed when we compare modern spectator sport—and certainly modern violent hero movies—with the ancient public worship practices of the Roman arena. But of course, a lot has changed. While people still die occasionally in professional sport (and sports such as motor racing are indeed pitching human skill against the ever-present risk of death), this is now accidental rather than central to the entertainment itself. Blood sports performed by heroes and villains of daemonic powers are now the domain of movies, of actors, and of carefully constructed special effects; live sport is not set up as requiring death any more. So in this context it is possible to simply be a great athlete where your day job is a public performer of physical prowess. Indeed, should one just happen to be incredibly dexterous and strong there is no reason why one could not love God and also be a professional sportsperson. However, the role of the hero, the place of spectacle entertainment in our culture, and the connections between financial and political power and the arena needs to be looked with a doxological eye before professional sport itself can be doxologically cleared.

When a sportsperson, a rock star, a celebrity, or a political leader becomes an idol—an object of personal and public veneration and adoration—they are performing a doxological function that is, by definition, idolatrous. How does this work? I myself am not any good at boxing, but should I treat a great athlete like Mohammad Ali or Mike Tyson as a hero to emulate and admire, I am seeking to vicariously participate in the dominating power and might of my hero. In Augustine's terms, this is the seduction of the daemonic. To aspire to a kind of immortal natural capacity embodying very mortal desires for power, desirability, and most importantly glory, this is to seek human significance in a source other than, as Kierkegaard puts it, "the separation of the religious individual before God in the responsibility of eternity." For victorious elitist greatness always comes at the competitive expense of those who one has proven to have bettered; this is glory defined by one's relative standing among one's peers. Glory is here inherently humanly defined, and it is a search for oneself without reference to God. It will not satisfy, but we set up norms and competitive systems and build religious frameworks around this idol and it becomes a unifying *religio* that sets up a false center of value and worth within the deep structures of how our society operates. This false center attracts other supportive false centers—the doxological centers of financial and political power—and so a system of false worship solidifies around us, and uses heroes and the adulation of the masses for those heroes.

THE AUGUSTINIAN CURE

Thinking along Augustine's trajectory, there is a two-step cure for the idolatry of professional sport: deliverance and the re-orienting of love.

Deliverance recognizes that we are doxological beings, such that we are built for right worship—that is, our bodies are temples. Our very beings are entities that are set up to be centered on some worth, some value-orienting core. So there must be a casting out of the false deity from our being if we are to be fit for the indwelling of the Holy Spirit.

The point of divine indwelling is the fulfillment and proper freedom of the human person. This is in contrast to the possession of our being by the dark gods of false worship, where bondage is inherent in this process as this is not what our Creator has made us to be. We can only freely be what we really are (what our Creator has called us into being to be) when our very being is a cleansed temple in which worship of the one true God is continuously enacted. So the indwelling of the Holy Spirit is entirely different to possession by daemonic powers; the former entails freedom from base desires and the elemental principles of the world, and true human fulfillment; the latter is a bondage to an increasingly sordid degradation of our own and other's dignity, which is bondage to habits, fears, the will to dominate, and lusts that control us and that can never bring true satisfaction.

The notion of deliverance is hard for us moderns to fathom because we tend to think of the self in Cartesian atomic terms. That is, we think that the only "I" that indwells my body is myself. Both Augustine and Kierkegaard are entirely unpersuaded by this atomic anatomy of the self, which is why the category of the daemonic makes such ready sense to them. The ontology Augustine and Kierkegaard work with maintains that the human self is not its own source and has no autonomous existence. This "I" is primitively grounded in the "thou" of God and only has reality in itself as a relation to its Divine Source. So daemonic possession is not something that happens to an atomic self that is invaded. Rather, the relational self—the self that is already a relation between the creature and the Creator—is promiscuously interfered with by another "god," falsely posing as the source and fulfillment of the "I." For this reason the Hebrew scriptures often describe idolatry as fornication. A relational anthropology of the "I" is assumed here where the worshipper is only conceivable as part of a covenantal relational entity—a marriage—rather than an atomic individual as such.

So deliverance entails the recognition and renunciation of false worship. This false worship is a distortion of the self, for the self can only freely be what it uniquely is in right relation with its Source—God. For this reason all heroes (sports figures no less than any other) must always be seen as potential seducers of the soul from its right source and destiny. And should we seek to vicariously construct the glory of our own self around the glory of a hero and their powers and desirability, or a nation, or—if we are any good in any competitive arena—our own prowess and achievements, we are spiritual fornicators who will need deliverance if we are to return to right worship, and to become both free and, as defined by our most primary ontic relation, ourself.

But what if we naturally excel at some sport, or have an outstanding talent for anything? Is being outstanding itself a doxological problem?

This is an interesting question. The very notion of elitism—the idea that one gains significance and value as a human being by being outstanding in some comparatively recognized way or another—is an inherently agonistic and competitive cult. The desire for fame, the desire to be recognized, the desire to be admired because one is outstanding at something—this is, as Kierkegaard fully appreciates, the desire to construct the self out of recognition from others, by (ironically) being just like then, only quantitatively better. The middle-class sport of the accumulation of possessions and power to display success also fits this model of competitive self-constructing idolatry.

All natural gifts are dangerous as potential sites of idolatry, but to the pure, all things are pure. That is, if the love of God is first, then all other loves and all human powers and giftings have their right and joyful place. Sport can be an act of worship that glorifies the Creator as much as any other human enterprise. Sport performed by decidedly non-elite sportsmen and woman for the sheer enjoyment of corporate venture and creative human movement is a great joy. Even competition, under this telos, can be fun and an expression of love. But the illusions of competitive worth—as if some of God's children are of more value than others because they have comparatively better extrinsic capacities in this or that arena of human endeavor—is an inherently corrupting tendency in any elite context that the Christian must strongly reject. Yet, if one's talents and one's development of those talents has led to outstanding prowess in any field of human endeavor, this, of course, should be an avenue for the joyful and humble worship of God. But a right attitude of worship is necessary to keep any elite display of human skill playful and enjoyable. If simply winning is what matters—and the institutions and financial interested embedded in elite sport are, alas, dominated by the idolatry of agonistic victor glory—then elite sport is not a good place to be. The way the community views sport and what vested commercial and political interests are integral with the spectacle of mass entertainment is a doxologically charged context that cannot be extracted from sport itself.

SHOPPING

I have titled this section shopping, but really I am interested in consumerism. What I mean by consumerism is a way of life centered on the goal of accumulating and consuming things and experiences in the attempt to construct a satisfied and meaningful life. This is a powerful doxological driver in our liberal secular life-world. Further, enormous marketing budgets are spent in order to form us to be ever more dedicated consumers so that we can be financially harvested in order to produce further financial power for those who engage in commerce.

I am not trying to suggest that commerce, advertising, and shopping are inherently bad things. But I do want to suggest that these things are never doxologically neutral. For example, businesses rely on good will, which is the accumulation of trust between the parties in commercial exchange. Trade practices are regulated to ensure that basic categories of trust in the public arena of trade are upheld. So the love of neighbor and the relational context of exchange are recognized in how trade actually works. Economies rely on trust or they don't work. Whether people buy and sell out of a love of neighbor and a trust in their neighbor that is merely instrumental, or one that upholds the intrinsic dignity of the neighbor, comes back to the manner in which love itself is understood and practiced in a public context. Love practiced in right piety—love practiced as a subsidiary feature of the love of God—is what ultimately facilitates a viable economy, whatever people's conscious theology or religion (or lack thereof) may be. Charlatans, con artists, and people who do not pay their bills are parasitic on the human trust and dignity that makes a functional trading economy viable. We will leave production out of things for the moment, though of course there the systemic exploitation of nature and cheap labor is only parasitic on the production foundations of the global economy in an ontological sense. Functionally, the violation of love of neighbor and the reckless exploitation of creation are foundational to how the most basic structures of global trade in goods and resources now work.[11] Equally, while the high finance world of currency trading and derivative trading is ontologically parasitic on the global economy, these parasites now have many orders of magnitude more financial power than the global trade in real goods and services. In her 2015 book, Susan George, using conservative, authoritative, public-access figures for 2014 from the Bank of International Settlements, points out that derivative trading was then running at $700 trillion US per annum, with currency trading running at a staggering $1,825 trillion US per annum. In comparison, the global GDP in real goods and services is estimated at a trivial $70 trillion US per annum.[12] Economics, jobs, and real trade in goods and services has got very little to do with real financial power now. Add to this the obscenity of financial secrecy jurisdictions shielding the global super-rich from tax at the very heart of our global financial system, the manner in which high-end corporations are above the law and bailed out by states when in trouble, and you can see that financial power has become entirely parasitic on the real needs and interests of the global majority.[13] What these deep inversions of actual economic reality indicate is that something is drastically awry at the doxological core of global financial and corporate power.

Yet, commerce is an inherently moral and doxological activity. Business is never simply about business, but if it is, that person or business cannot be trusted or traded with in any fair or sustainable way. So commerce is a doxologically situated activity that can only finally work where the two great commandments—to love

11. See Goff, *Mammon's Ecology*.

12. George, *Shadow Sovereigns*, 25.

13. Shaxson, *Treasure Islands*; Garrett, *Too Big To Fail*; Ferguson, *Inside Job*. It is fascinating to look at the profoundly different logic of medieval economics, which certainly was not as "efficient" as modern markets, precisely because things like just price, moral principles, quality, trust and community service, were central to how economic and financial concerns were governed. See Wood, *Medieval Economic Thought*.

God first and to love one's neighbor as oneself—are at least to some extent in place. Let us take that as given and move on to look at how the worship core of shopping is loaded toward the wrong center.

Let us enter the doxological sociology of shopping via Christmas and birthday presents. Santa is a child-formation myth that reinforces consumerism as a viable center of worth around which our children can construct meaning and significance in their lives. Christmas and birthdays provide parents with an opportunity to affirm their love for their children and affirm the value and significance of each child's own sense of self-worth, by giving them things. The message picked up is that one is affirmed as valuable and significant as the owner of new things. This is highly unlikely to be the parent's intention, but could it be that this is largely what children are actually formed to believe via these significant social rituals, because the false doxological promise of consumerism is what our larger cultural world has formed our *adults* to believe, and they are unconsciously replicating their own formation onto their children?

The reason why I think this is the case is that our culture has largely accepted a functional public materialism as true. This has undermined the higher meaning of gifts and festivals such that gifts and festivals can now only *really* be about things and pleasurable experiences, and now things and experiences only *really* have meaning as the means of power, pleasure, and identity-affiliation. This undermines the intrinsic dignity of the human soul and the sacramental significance of bonded relationships (love) such that an insatiable avarice for the acquisition of things becomes a deep yet inherently inadequate carrier of human significance in our cultural context.

Again, the Augustinian cure for this is deliverance and ecclesially supported, rightly ordered love. We have gone over deliverance above in relation to hero worship, but here let us look a little more closely at ecclesially supported, rightly ordered love in relation to consumerism.

THE CHURCH AS A DOXOLOGICAL
HABITUS FOR LOVE

In *The City of God*, Augustine points out that the central difference between the City of Man and the City of God is the first object of desire. The City of Man is doxologically structured around the love of glory, which is *self*-love. The City of God is doxologically structured around the love and God and the love of neighbor *before* the love of self.

In Augustine's way of understanding human society, it is taken as given that the normal inclinations of our desires are malformed by the doxologically distorted fallen habitus that we are born into. The reform of our desire such that we can love God first, and hence rightly order all secondary loves, is central to what Christian practice actually entails. But desire is integral with habit in practice such that we develop good habits that facilitate right worship and healthy loves by being willing participants in a disciplined community committed to those ends. That community, for the Christian, is the church.

In the context of our consumer society, how can the church be a habitus for right desire?

There are a number of serious obstacles we must recognize. Firstly, we are formed by consumer society *not* to have disciplines that control our consumption desires. Very clever marketing psychologists and advertising firms conspire to bypass rational discipline in relation to purchasing, and go straight for our needs, fears, and desires.[14] The ready availability of credit conspires with commercial interests. Powerful desire-priming and the easy means of immediate satisfaction are forming us in our personal shopping contexts all the time. This is not a fair contest, particularly for children, particularly when they are embedded in communication devices that are integral with algorithmic monitoring and sales engines, and where these devices themselves are designed to be use-addictive. This is the formation-saturation environment we live in 24/7, but we may only go to a church service for one hour a week.

14. See Packard, *Hidden Persuaders*; Klein, *No Logo*.

Secondly, as mentioned earlier, there is a fictive structure to our life-world where the religious, the spiritual, and the doxological is held to be discrete from the practical, the public, and the tangibly real. So the manner in which desire-formation is falsely held to be discrete from worship means that both secular atheists and religious believers do not recognize desire-formation towards the supreme good of consumerism (freedom to have whatever we want—self-love) as doxological in nature.

Thirdly, as William Cavanaugh points out, we are blind to the manner in which the holy migrates from properly sacral contexts to secular imitations of the sacred.[15] The nation takes on a public sacredness as first loyalty to God becomes a non-issue in the public square. Sex between free consenting adults comes to replace the sacrament of marriage as the deep site of relational meaning. Here any form of consenting sex—while explicitly secularized and while its meaning is explicitly constructed—becomes a de facto sacramental carrier of identity and meaning. Quantities (of money), power, and pleasure come to be sites of worship defining who we are, such that means, measures, and consequences become ends in themselves and the center of worth becomes savagely instrumentally and numerically distorted. So false worship is embedded in our lives if we are not true worshippers. For there is no neutral place outside of worship: we are worshiping beings.

To counter these things the church must have many responses. Her liturgies of worship cannot be shaped by consumer culture; marketing tricks and merely emotive appeals to base desires and fears cannot be harvested to promote success or relevance in the terms of consumer culture. Yet as important as corporate worship is, this is a very small part of the formation of the church in terms of habitus. The ordinary daily context of our habits and desire-formations are where the church must be a powerful community, helping shape our desires and worship in accordance with the doxological center of the City of God. Here families and friends supporting each other in common habits and meaningful rituals of good worship-formation are vital. If the worship of the liturgy does

15. Cavanaugh, *Migrations of the Holy.*

not translate into our personal, familial, friendship, and working habits of being, then it has no real impact on the doxological shape of our lives and will not hold out long from the very powerful, false doxological-formation currents of the culture in which we swim.

We must recognize that we are being deeply and relentlessly doxologically formed towards self-love by our consumer society. This is a problem for adults but it is a particular problem for children. All the time they are being asked, "What do you want?" as if their personal gratification, in the terms they choose, is what is best for them and for us all. Worse, their social world is now mediated to them by functionally narcissistic technological interfaces that re-shape their neural process to function without the usual interactive social norms governing give-and-take between real people.[16] So children can be very technologically "connected" to their peers, but it is a connection that is on and off as they choose and controlled entirely by their own interest-horizons, and tends towards a sort of collective narcissism rather than real community. They are typically *not* connected to their parents as often enough peer-to-peer communication replaces other social bonds (parents do this too). The manner in which iPhones, video games, social media, and simply a computer interface are great baby sitters for parents (and teachers) re-enforces a bubble world of self-love as increasingly the social norm in family settings.[17]

These trends have to be faced and fought. Micro-family practices are the first line of defense, but families need communities that stand with them against the powerful and ubiquitous self-love-formation currents of our times. Healthy family micro-rituals that form us to love God and each other before our selves—saying grace, family devotions, eating together, doing domestic jobs together, going to church together—these need to be seen as of crucial significance to the daily life of the church. Getting phones, screens, and TVs out of the relational spaces of our family lives so that we can give proper attention to the people we actually live

16. See Greenfield, *Mind Change*; Schmidt, *Between Stimulus and Response*.

17. See Lasch, *The Culture of Narcissism*.

with, and care directly for each other; these are now deeply doxologically subversive acts. If we make no effort not to go with the flow of our times, then we will be atomized and narcisized and devoted to the pursuit of our own gratification, just as the powerful forces of consumer society desire.

The church needs to be seen as a community of believers who are regularly gathered around the worship of God and then sent out into the world as agents of subversion of the false doxological center (self-love) that defines the City of Man. But actually, colonization in the reverse direction is always a threat. We are in constant need of support and formation in the love of God and neighbor above the love of self, as everything in our larger life-world is geared towards the love of self as the obvious doxological core of our common life.

Churches readily concede to the tacit doxological norms of the larger culture. Our worship must be emotionally gratifying, we segregate the children and youth from the adults just as our larger society does, we offer fun and appealing programs for special-interest groups, we accept the discretely personal and moral horizon of religious faith offered to us by secular modernity. Thus, the secularized, self-pleasing, interest-group-atomizing, and individual-freedom-focused norms of our consumer society shape our ministry without us even noticing it.

We need to see the church as the community that forms and supports us in the Christian habits of love—the love of God and neighbor over the love of self. This community needs to have its own distinctive rituals, habits, and language of love, in some ways like a cultural ghetto, which is different from the larger culture that has its habits of love defined by a different doxological core to what we profess allegiance to. Christian habits and rituals need to be a constant habitus that we inhabit and support each other in inhabiting. This is a way of being that cannot be discretely religious and personal, for love is inherently relational and—dare I say it—inherently public. Because God so loved the world we also must express our love for God and neighbor in the world. But we cannot let the world define our love, for its love is idolatrous.

TECHNOLOGY

I have titled this section "technology" rather than "power," but our technologies always seem to have a tacit formation tendency towards the worship of power. To be clear, that we are tool makers and users, and that power can be an instrumental good are not things I wish to deny or in any way belittle. But doxologically, power is always seductive. And it is, again, a doxological seduction towards self-love over the love of God and neighbor.

Let us think a little about how our technologies shape, instrumentalize, and change us, and to what doxological end these changes seem to be tending in our times.

Firstly, by now it should be clear that no aspect of the mode of life in which we live is doxologically neutral. Here we hit immediately on the great lie of modern technology: its mere instrumental neutrality. There are deep historical reasons why we tend to believe this obvious sociological and theological nonsense. These reasons are tied back to what is now a quite fabulous mythology of the birth of the modern scientific age. But the fact is, we have an instrumental conception of technological power because of an enormous metaphysical revolution that coincides with and deeply shaped the Scientific Revolution.

To recap very briefly, modern science has a functionally materialist outlook on nature. That is, our science is a reductive and deterministic type of knowledge derived from the careful observation of physical phenomena and the mathematical formulation of necessary or statistically probable laws of causal behavior.[18] This knowledge gives us wonderful insight into how things physically work and how we can manipulate the way things work so that we

---

18. Actually, science is an imaginative enterprise conducted by communities of knowers, as Michael Polanyi points out beautifully in *Personal Knowledge*. That is science is a very rich human endeavor, and has often been understood as a form of contemplative worship by scientists who are Christians. Even so, the *meaning* of scientific knowledge is more or less structurally separated from the *method* and *content* of scientific knowledge within modernity, such that it is fair to say that modern scientific knowledge itself is understood to be functionally materialist, reductively rationalist, and mechanically determinist.

can gain power over some aspects of physical nature. This knowledge, as applied in technology, has transformed our world and the way we live beyond recognition. It has transformed our relation to the natural world, our relation to work, our social and personal relations, our commerce, religion, communications, bureaucracies, entertainment, warfare, and our politics. Science (*scientia*) and technology always did this, but since the seventeenth century it has done this at an ever-accelerating speed and a life-world-reconfiguring depth that is unprecedented.[19] It is because of the impact of modern technology that sacred established stabilities of social order are now almost impossible to maintain.

Even though modern warfare is horrifically destructive and our technological way of life is well on the way to crashing the natural balances of the biosphere, our cultural attitude towards technology is largely positive and determinist (even eschatological). There is a doxological reason for this. We believe that no problem that might arise cannot be solved simply by the development of greater technological power. That is, we have enormous faith, as mentioned earlier, in the Principality of Man.

Since Francis Bacon in the seventeenth century, the mastery of nature by scientific knowledge has been seen as the key to progressing the human condition. The wondrous success of science and technology backs up this progressive story. But another shift has accompanied this practical success. In our academies the very idea of truth has become defined by the reductively material, mathematical, and instrumental categories of modern science and technology. Intelligence, quality, and transcendence have disappeared as real features of the world and have been replaced by reductively factual knowledge and instrumental know-how. This, negatively, gives us enormously powerful instrumental *scientia* (knowledge) but no matching *sapientia* (wisdom) that could guide our knowledge and power to genuinely good ends. Positively, it puts us in the place of God. When there is really no such thing as religious or moral truth—but only factual truth and instrumental power—we are our own arbiters and constructors of all value and

19. McNeill, *The Great Acceleration.*

116

meaning. This, indeed, is seen by progressives as a coming of age, as a cultural maturing, when we cast off the superstitious unscientific beliefs of humanity's childhood and boldly make value and meaning up for ourselves.

A culturally assumed progressive vision of the glory of a self-created person is intimately tangled up in our love of new technologies and our blindness to their (and our) destructive tendencies. This tacit worship orientation is as ubiquitous and unnoticed in our culture as is the self-love doxological tendency of modern consumerism. But we should notice it as Christians and we should have an understanding of the nature, use, and saving power of technology that is not framed by a tacit doxological fealty to the Principality of Man.

Technology, then, is not religiously neutral. It is not a mere instrumentality that, in itself, is neither good nor bad. Power always has a theological orientation. The theological power question is, are we subjects of the Ruler of Heaven and Earth and seeking to orient our worship around the great commandments, or are we masters of our own destiny, thanks to our own powers, and hence orienting our worship around self-love? The way we answer this doxological question will decide whether the technology itself is a largely good or bad one, and whether the use of any given technology (be it a good- or bad-oriented technology) is for a good or bad end. We are not used to thinking about technology in this manner. We would rather assume a so-called realist and supposedly theologically neutral (or a-theological) stance where if the power exists, someone will use it, so we had better create the power first and make sure that we use it for what we decide is in our best interest. But clearly, this type of realism is not theologically neutral—it is embedded in the doxological life-world defined by self-love.

RELIGION AND THE GOSPEL

Today, it is not hard to find very penetrating and powerful socio-politically situated theological critiques of religion.[20] As his late writings clearly show, Kierkegaard would be in full sympathy with this outlook. The strong message of this literature is that religion is inherently man-made, sinful, and also totally inextricable from communal life and personal consciousness. Yet, when a theologians points this out, its meaning is almost exactly the opposite of when a functionally materialist social scientists points out that—to commandeer Nietzsche's astonishing turn of phrase—religion is human, all too human. The point of a theological critique of religion is to raise profound doxological cautions against idolatry in all religious contexts, be those contexts commonly deemed to be sacred or profane. The insight here is that religion—unifying collective beliefs, institutions, myths, narratives, practices, knowledge systems, power structures, and moralities—are inextricable from our existence as human beings. Religion is ubiquitous, it is not discretely sacral, and yet the sacred, however that is designated, is the focus of highest value, and is at the core of the religious. *Re*-ligion is always the treating of a wound, the attempt to *re*bind that which is fragmented, disjointed, and alienated from the head of the true civic body and the very heart of each self within community. This, Christian faith entirely understands. So there is no surprise that violence, exploitation, powerful irrational fears and desires, and the endlessly weeping wound of alienation between the soul, the Divine, creation, others, and the self is inescapable, not just in religion, but in the human condition before the eschaton. This weeping wound defines both the darkest tragedy and the most glorious hope of what it means to be human. Thus, we yearn

---

20. For some significant theological texts on the sociological nature of religion, in recent times, from different ecclesial traditions, see: Girard, *Violence and the Sacred*; Ellul, *Subversion of Christianity*; Yannaras, *Against Religion*; Barth, *On Religion*; Budde, *The (Magic) Kingdom of God*. All of these thinkers have complex understandings of both the pitfalls and the inevitability of religion in all socio-cultural contexts (including, in the modern sense, religious contexts).

and travail with the whole of creation, as in labor, waiting for the birth of the healed world. All the religious energies of humanity are continuously strivings to overcome this primal alienation, to re-bind these grating separations into which we simply find ourselves existentially thrown. And yet, our strivings never succeed.

So let us not think of religion as some discrete part of our lives, and as something that some people do not choose to participate in. This is an impossibility. What should concern us is the life-long struggle to cast off the natural idolatry of the fallen human condition, a struggle in which all of us participate all of the time. The religious structures that bind us to the fallen normality of every worldly context will have less hold over us (and we will become more problematic to that world) the freer from disordered first love we can become. This becoming is a pilgrimage, and progress is only possible via the work of the Holy Spirit within each individual before God, and in the collective habitus of the community of believers seeking the kingdom of God. And the gospel, the good news, is that that which is impossible for us is possible for God. And so we strive towards an eschaton we ourselves cannot make happen. This is the theological meaning of hope.[21]

---

21. See Moltmann, *Theology of Hope* for what is still one of the best recent expressions of this enduring Christian truth.

Conclusion

Kierkegaard's Prophetic Fire
for the Present Age

THE PROPHETIC FIRE OF Kierkegaard's *Two Ages* is this: because Kierkegaard has the type of theological outlook that grants him a clear understanding of the primary, existentially causal categories of human belief and action, he can see why the Present Age arises and he understands what it really is. This understanding gives him his extraordinary ability to chart the trajectory of the Present Age, not only of his time, but into our time, and beyond. So keen is his knowledge that—by inference—we are able to see how the Present Age will end as well. Conversely, without an understanding of the inner religious dynamics that govern the norms of the Present Age, false dystopia, false optimism, or fundamental perplexity are the only ways of understanding the deep drivers and final destinations of the Present Age.

False dystopias understand the dynamics of social evolution in an entirely naturalistic manner such that mere instrumental power can replace or obliterate the human spirit. This is a common theme of American apocalyptic movies. This stance is profoundly bleak because it functionally assumes that the human spirit does not exist, that the relation of the soul to God that causes the human spirit does not exist, and that God does not exist. Here the logic of mere instrumental power comes to displace humanity entirely in the forward projection of present trends. But such outlooks are not realistic if what Kierkegaard means by "the religious" is indeed the most primary feature of human existence. There will be spiritual sedation, cultural banalization, the destruction of democracy by public relations, powerful lobby groups, and ever-more-cunning marketing techniques, and all of this will indeed be driven by powerful economic interests backed by the forces of violence entrusted to the modern state in order to preserve the status quo. But such a trajectory has its limits on a number of fronts. Firstly, the insatiable priming of consumer desire and the relentless imperative for the growth of mere financial power, assumes the interminable ongoing viability of an ever-increasing level of human and natural exploitation, which can simply not be sustained. Secondly, as Kierkegaard brilliantly explores, the very satisfactions that make the public a willing partner in its own bondage are in fact false satisfactions—they are expressions of despair. A culture cannot sustain its optimism and vitality where despair is its life-form's background ethos. So when the unsustainable exploitations on which the Present Age is premised give out, then two things happen. The background level of despair in the common person surges to the fore (for his or her sedations and distractions are removed), and the means of protecting privilege revert to overt forms of violence. Such an anguished social life-form can survive for some time, but it cannot ultimately settle down into a stable equilibrium. The human spirit will not accept suppression and despair forever. Thus, dystopia where technological means enable the crushing of the human spirit forever cannot, finally, be produced.[1] Dystopia where

1. See Orwell, *Nineteen Eighty-Four*. As wonderfully stimulating as this classic text is, the idea that the perfectly rational system of instrumental power—and power that exists entirely for its own sake—could forever tread on the face of humanity does not take into account that it must be humans who run any social machinery of exploitation. But why the spite against humanity? And how would that spite be maintained once the perfect system of perpetual oppression was established? Perhaps Orwell is actually hinting at a demonic resentment that possesses the human mediums of oppressive power. But this places the dynamic of causality back in the arena of the war of heaven where, as Arthur Millar put it in *The Crucible*, "Heaven and Hell do wrestle on our backs." This puts the analysis back in the arena of religion and here humanity and its powers are not the ultimate and final realities.

natural and political disaster leads to anarchic violence such that the entire globe is burnt up in a fire storm of perpetual war is again, something the human soul—with all its powers of violence and cruelty—is not, finally, capable of achieving.[2] As deeply embedded as sin is in our human condition, the Good—as Plato expresses it—is more fundamental. As prone as sinful human nature is to war, peace—as Augustine expresses it—is the ontological reality in which the struggle of creation, ontologically bruised by death, is embedded. If Kierkegaard is right then dystopian despair prophesying the obliteration of the human spirit is a terrifying nihilistic nightmare, yet it is also strangely hubristic and it is not grounded in the fundamentals of human reality.

Equally, false optimism is ungrounded. There is indeed something profoundly diseased about the cultural norms of the Present Age, and no amount of wiz-bang gadgetry or social engineering or political ideology or romantic optimism will fix that. Science, economics, and politics will not save us. The internet, Twitter, Facebook, iPad, iPhones, technological innovation, more information, more economic growth—these will not save us, and they are all essentially distractions from our core problem. While corporate reform, ethical shopping, sustainable land use, farming practice reforms, environmental responsibility, renewable energy, and such like, are all good things—none of these things in themselves address the cause of our civilizational malaise. Any attempted ethical

2. See William Shakespeare's *Macbeth*. The religious and moral horizon that gives rise to the soul of this play's tragic villain cannot be overthrown in defiance of those realities, and the defiance itself causes ruin to the villain in the very performance of his evil acts. With powerful insight, Shakespeare depicts the deceptions in the false promise to satisfy the desire for power which constitutes Macbeth's temptation. Moral and religious realities can be ignored and defied for a time, but in the universe where these realities are primary, victory won by violent and immoral force is a victory that ultimately brings greater harm to the victor than to the vanquished. Dante's *Divine Comedy* illustrates this same perspective. This is not a perspective in any manner naive about human evil or unaware of the relentless tendency towards the abuse of human power. Yet this understanding of human motivation and of the frames of spiritual reality upon which human action and value is premised is what gives Shakespeare's works so much greater depth and existential realism than modern visions of the psyche that are constructed in entirely *naturalistic* terms.

reform pursued within the ethos of the Present Age will be seriously undermined by the sub-human logic and religiously impoverished spirituality of the age. The cause of our deep proclivity to unfixable ethical illnesses is doxological, and trying to treat the ethical symptoms of our malaise will not affect a lasting cure for our ethical problems.

Fundamental perplexity is the best our spiritually undiscerning outlook on the causal drivers of society in the Present Age can give us. I recall listening to some very intelligent journalists perplexedly wondering what has happened to democratic politics under the conditions of the highly managed public relations machinery that government is now embedded in the mass-media age.[3] The obvious truth, which Ellul pointed out in the 1960s, is that democracy is, in the end, simply incompatible with the ever-more efficient techniques of manipulating public opinion that mass society governed by the mindset of *la technique* calls into being. But where there is no frame of thinking about the *drivers* of society other than functionally materialist, functionally atheistic frames, then where this impasse will take us and what it means remains entirely opaque.

Christ tells us that "in this world you will have trouble. But take heart, I have overcome the world" (John 16:33). This is both the soul of clear-eyed realism and the source of hope. This combination of realism and hope alone can gives us the motivation to pursue right worship and the Good, here and now—however hopeless a good outcome from our actions might actually be in our own life times. C. S. Lewis spells this dynamic of practical hope out beautifully. It is worth quoting at some length:

> Hope is one of the Theological virtues. This means that a continual looking forward to the eternal world is not (as some modern people think) a form of escapism or wishful thinking, but one of the things a Christian is meant to do. It does not mean that we are to leave the present

3. Australian Broadcasting Corporation, Radio National, "Late Night Live with Phillip Adams," 27 May 2013: http://www.abc.net.au/radionational/programs/latenightlive/people-and-the-politics---usa-and-australia/4712288.

world as it is. If you read your history you will find that the Christians who did most for the present world were just those who thought most of the next. The Apostles themselves, who set on foot the conversion of the Roman Empire, the great men who built up the Middle Ages, the English Evangelicals who abolished the Slave Trade, all left their mark on Earth, precisely because their minds were occupied with Heaven. It is since Christians have largely ceased to think of the other world that they have become so ineffective in this. Aim at Heaven and you will get earth thrown in: aim at earth and you will get neither.[4]

So rather than dystopian despair, naïve optimism, or paralyzing perplexity, a vision of Christ and confidence in his triumph over all that bruises the world, as revealed in his own Passion, can motivate our hearts and minds towards right worship and the actions of love and suffering that right worship requires in the context of the world. But to do this we cannot let our vision be shaped by a this-world-alone horizon; the very horizon of the classical social sciences, the self-love, and the instrumental-power realism of our age. And, actually, that flatly reductive vision can't see what is *really* going on in the social world anyway, for it is blind to that which is most fundamental in all social contexts: the seriousness—or lack thereof—of the individual before the responsibility of eternity.

Kierkegaard's doxological sociology, then, is a prophetic fire in a number of senses. Firstly, it burns down the false pretenses of a mere materialist conception of sociological, psychological, and political human dynamics. Secondly, it is a fire of judgment. The Present Age is an idolatrous age. There is nothing new about any age being an idolatrous age, but no age likes to hear this truth. The prouder the age the less inclined towards conviction and repentance that age is. And we are a proud age. Through the hubris of the Principality of Man, particularly as expressed in our secular, materialist, and pragmatic-knowledge culture, we deem ourselves to have progressed beyond the cultural immaturities of religion. We have built our liberal secular and technological life-world

4. Lewis, *Mere Christianity*, 134.

around this hubris, and so the very idea of idolatry is either in-comprehensible to us, or embraced by atheistic humanists as a sign of maturity. And it must be faced, this hubris of the Principality of Man is alive and well within our churches. As always, judg-ment starts with the house of God. If those outside of the house of Christian faith, or those who have thrown off faith out of disgust with the house of God, are idolaters, that is only natural. But if we who claim to worship the true God are blind to our own idolatry and determined to set up alters to the idols of our times in our churches and in our own hearts, this cannot end well for us. But thirdly, Kierkegaard's theological sociology is a warming hearth fire for the communion of saints, that can rekindle the theological virtue of hope and the proper scope of theology in our times. This courageous, infuriating, cantankerous, and profoundly passionate Dane can remind us of the obvious dynamics of the social world, and draw us back to the deep resources of Christian theology in understanding the world in which we live. Should we receive the Gadfly's bite, this would do us the world of good.

If the arguments in this little book are some way towards be-ing correct, then the interesting conclusion of the matter seems to be that it takes someone who is not defined by the spirit of the Present Age to realistically and deeply understand this age. In more New Testament terms, one might even say that its takes someone who is not of the world to really understand the world. Thus, Kierkegaard is a clear-eyed, this-world-concerned prophet for our times, even though he lived so long ago. Let us follow his lead and think about our social context through a doxological lens, and pursue the practice of right worship in all humility, as best as we can, in every context in which we find ourselves.

Bibliography

Adams, Phillip. "Late Night Live with Phillip Adams." Australian Broadcasting Corporation, Radio National, 27 May 2013: http://www.abc.net.au/radionational/programs/latenightlive/people-and-the-politics—-usa-and-australia/4712288

Alighieri, Dante. *Divine Comedy*. 3 vols. London: Penguin, 1949, 1955, 1962.

Asad, Talal. *Formations of the Secular*. Palto Alto, CA: Stanford University Press, 2003.

———. *Genealogies of Religion*. Baltimore: John Hopkins University Press, 1993.

Augustine. *City of God*. London: Penguin Classics, 1984.

———. *The Confessions of Saint Augustine*. London: Hodder & Stoughton, 1983.

———. "Seventh Homily on the First Epistle of John." In *Nicene and Post-Nicene Fathers*, Vol. VII, edited by Philip Schaff, 501–5. Edinburgh: T. & T. Clark, 1991.

———. *Of True Religion*. In *Augustine: Early Writings*, edited and translated by J. H. S. Burleigh, 225–83. Louisville, KY: Westminster John Knox, 2006.

Bacon, Francis. *New Atlantis and The Great Instantiation*. Chichester, UK: Wiley-Blackwell, 2012.

Barth, Karl. *On Religion: The Revelation of God as the Sublimation of Religion*. London: T. & T. Clark, 2006.

Berger, Peter L., and Thomas Luckmann. *The Social Construction of Reality*. London: Penguin, 1971.

Berger, Peter L., ed. *The Desecularization of the World*. Grand Rapids: Eerdmans, 1999.

———. *Facing Up to Modernity*. London: Penguin, 1977.

Betz, John R. *After Enlightenment: Hamann as Post-Secular Visionary*. Chichester, UK: Wiley-Blackwell, 2009.

Bonhoeffer, Dietrich. *Ethics*. New York: Simon & Schuster, 1995.

Brueggemann, Walter. *Money and Possessions*. Louisville: Westminster John Knox, 2016.

———. *The Prophetic Imagination*. Minneapolis: Fortress, 2001.

Bibliography

Budde, Michael. *The (Magic) Kingdom of God: Christianity and Global Culture Industries*. Boulder, CO: Westview, 1998.

Campolo, Anthony. *The Power Delusion*. Wheaton, IL: Victor, 1986.

Cavanaugh, William T. *Migrations of the Holy: God, State, and the Political Meaning of the Church*. Grand Rapids: Eerdmans, 2011.

——. *The Myth of Religious Violence*. Oxford: Oxford University Press, 2009.

Clark, Manning. *A Short History of Australia*. London: Penguin, 2006.

Das, Satyajit. *Extreme Money: The Masters of the Universe and the Cult of Risk*. New Jersey: FT Press, 2011.

Desmond, William. *The Intimate Strangeness of Being*. Washington, DC: The Catholic University of America Press, 2012.

Draper, John William. *History of the Conflict between Religion and Science*. Cambridge: Cambridge University Press, 2009.

Dupré, Louis. *Passage to Modernity*. New Haven: Yale University Press, 1993.

Durkheim, Émile. *The Elementary Forms of the Religious Life*. Oxford: Oxford University Press, 2008.

Ellul, Jacques. *Money and Power*. Basingstoke, UK: Marshall Pickering, 1986.

——. *Propaganda*. New York: Vintage, 1973.

——. *The Subversion of Christianity*. Grand Rapids: Eerdmans, 1986.

——. *The Technological Society*. New York: Vintage, 1965.

Evans, C. Stephen. *Passionate Reason*. Indianapolis: Indiana University Press, 1992.

——. *Søren Kierkegaard's Christian Psychology*. Vancouver, BC: Regent College, 1990.

Ferguson, Charles. *Inside Job: The Financiers Who Pulled Off the Heist of the Century*. London: One World, 2012.

Feuerbach, Ludwig. *The Essence of Christianity*. New York: Harper & Row, 1957.

Frankfurt, Harry G. *On Bullshit*. Princeton: Princeton University Press, 2005.

Garff, Joakim. *Søren Kierkegaard: A Biography*. Princeton: Princeton University Press, 2005.

Garrett, Brandon L. *Too Big to Fail: How Prosecutors Compromise with Corporations*. Cambridge: Harvard University Press, 2014.

George, Susan. *Shadow Sovereigns: How Global Corporations are Seizing Power*. Cambridge: Polity, 2015.

Gerson, Lloyd P. *Ancient Epistemology*. Cambridge: Cambridge University Press, 2009.

Girard, René. *Violence and the Sacred*. Baltimore: John Hopkins University Press, 1979.

Goff, Stan. *Mammon's Ecology: Metaphysics of the Empty Sign*. Eugene, OR: Cascade, 2018.

Gomez, R. J. "What Is This Thing Called Philosophy of Technology?" www.eolss.net/Sample-Chapters/C05/E6-89-23-00.pdf

Greenfield, Susan. *Mind Change: How Digital Technologies Are Leaving Their Mark on Our Brains*. London: Penguin, 2014.

Bibliography

Gregory, Brad S. *The Unintended Reformation*. Cambridge: Harvard University Press, 2012.

Guardini, Romano. *The End of the Modern World*. Wilmington, DE: ISI, 1993.

Hamilton, Clive., Christopher Bonneuil, and François Gemenne. *The Anthropocene and the Global Environmental Crisis*. New York: Routledge, 2015.

Harrison, Peter. *The Territories of Science and Religion*. Chicago: Chicago University Press, 2015.

Hart, David Bentley. *The Experience of God*. New Haven: Yale University Press, 2014.

Henry, Michel. *Barbarism*. 2nd ed, New York: Continuum, 2012.

Heschel, Abraham. *The Prophets*. Peabody, MA: Hendrickson, 2009.

Horkheimer, Max., and Theodor Adorno. *Dialectic of Enlightenment*. New York: Continuum, 1993.

Jaensch, Dean. *The Hawk-Keating Hijack*. Sydney: Allen & Unwin, 1989.

Josephson-Storm, Jason A. *The Myth of Disenchantment: Magic, Modernity, and the Birth of the Human Sciences*. Chicago: University of Chicago Press, 2017.

Joy, Lynn Sumida. *Gassendi the Atomist*. Cambridge: Cambridge University Press, 2002.

Kant, Immanuel. *Critique of Pure Reason*. London: Everyman, 1993.

Kierkegaard, Søren. *Attack on "Christendom."* Princeton, NJ: Princeton University Press, 1944.

———. *Christian Discourses*. Princeton, NJ: Princeton University Press, 1997.

———. *Concluding Unscientific Postscript*. Princeton, NJ: Princeton University Press, 1992.

———. *Philosophical Fragments*. Princeton, NJ: Princeton University Press, 1985.

———. *The Sickness unto Death*. Princeton, NJ: Princeton University Press, 1980.

———. *Two Ages*. Princeton, NJ: Princeton University Press, 1978.

Klein, Naomi. *No Logo*. London: Flamingo, 2000.

Kluver, Randolph. "Jacques Ellul: Technique, Propaganda, and Modern Media." In *Perspectives on Culture, Technology and Communication*, edited by Casey Man Kong Lum, 97–116. New York: Hampton, 2005.

Kuhn, T. H. *The Structure of Scientific Revolutions*. Chicago: Chicago University Press, 1970.

Lasch, Christopher. *The Culture of Narcissism*. New York: Norton, 1991.

Latour, Bruno. *We Have Never Been Modern*. Cambridge: Harvard University Press, 1993.

Lewis, C. S. *Mere Christianity*. New York: HarperOne, 2001.

Malantschuk, Gregor. *The Controversial Kierkegaard*. Waterloo, ON: Wilfrid Laurier University Press, 1980.

Bibliography

Malesic, Jonathan. "Illusion and Offense in Philosophical Fragments: Kierkegaard's Inversion of Feuerbach's Critique of Christianity." *International Journal for Philosophy of Religion* 62.1 (2007) 43–55.

McNeil, John., and Peter Engelke. *The Great Acceleration*. Cambridge: Harvard University Press, 2014.

Milbank, John. *Theology and Social Theory*. 2nd ed. Oxford: Blackwell, 2006.

Miller, Arthur. *The Crucible*. London: Penguin, 1976.

Moltmann, Jürgen. *Theology of Hope*. Minneapolis: Fortress, 1993.

Nietzsche, Friedrich. *Beyond Good and Evil*. New York: Dover, 1997.

Northcott, Michael S. *A Political Theology of Climate Change*. London: SPCK, 2014.

Oliver, Simon. *Creation: A Guide for the Perplexed*. London: Bloomsbury, 2017.

Oreskes, Naomi., and Erik N. Conway. *Merchants of Doubt: How a Handful of Scientists Obscured the Truth on Issues from Tobacco Smoke to Global Warming*. London: Bloomsbury, 2011.

Orwell, George. *Nineteen Eighty-Four*. London: Penguin, 1954.

Packard, Vance. *The Hidden Persuaders*. London: Penguin, 1981.

Pasnau, Robert. *Metaphysical Themes 1274–1671*. Oxford: Oxford University Press, 2013.

Pérez-Álvarez, Eliseo. *A Vexing Gadfly: The Late Kierkegaard on Economic Matters*. Eugene, OR: Pickwick, 2009.

Phillips, D. Z. *Faith and Philosophical Enquiry*. London: Routledge, 1970.

Plato. *Complete Works*. Cambridge: Hackett, 1997.

Polanyi, Michael. *Personal Knowledge: Towards a Post-Critical Philosophy*. Chicago: University of Chicago Press, 1958.

Pusey, Michael. *Economic Rationalism in Canberra: A National Building State Changes Its Mind*. Cambridge: Cambridge University Press, 1991.

———. *The Experience of Middle Australia: The Dark Side of Economic Reform*. Cambridge: Cambridge University Press, 2003.

Ross, Chanon. *Gifts Glittering and Poisoned: Spectacle, Empire, and Metaphysics*. Eugene, OR: Cascade, 2014.

Rubenstein, Richard E. *Aristotle's Children: How Christians, Muslims, and Jews Rediscovered Ancient Wisdom and Illuminated the Middle Ages*. New York: Harvest, 2003.

Serreze, Mark. *Brave New Arctic: The Untold Story of the Melting North*. Princeton, NJ: Princeton University Press, 2018.

Schmidt, Peter. *Between Stimulus and Response: What Parents Need to Know about Electronic Screens and Kids*. Charlottesville, VA: Schmidt, 2016.

Shakespeare, William. *Complete Works*. Oxford: Clarendon, 2005.

Shaxson, Nicholas. *Treasure Islands: Tax Havens and the Men Who Stole the World*. London: Vintage, 2012.

Smith, Ronald Gregor. *J. G. Hamann*. London: Collins, 1960.

Smith, Wilfred Cantwell. *The Meaning and End of Religion*. Minneapolis: Fortress, 1991.

Bibliography

Strauss, David Friedrich. *The Life of Jesus Critically Examined*. Cambridge: Cambridge University Press, 2010.

Tanner, Michael. *Nietzsche: A Very Short Introduction*. Oxford: Oxford University Press, 2000.

Taylor, Charles. *A Secular Age*. Cambridge: Harvard University Press, 2007.

Tucker, Robert C., ed. *The Marx-Engels Reader*. London: Norton, 1978.

Tyson, Paul. *Returning to Reality: Christian Platonism for Our Times*. Eugene, OR: Cascade, 2014.

Varoufakis, Yanis. *The Global Minotaur: America, Europe and the Future of the Global Economy*. London: Zed, 2013.

Van Krieken, Robert., Philip Smith, Daphne Habibis, Kevin McDonald, Michael Haralambos, and Martin Holborn. *Sociology: Themes and Perspectives*. 2nd ed. Sydney: Longman, 2000.

Virilio, Paul. *The Administration of Fear*. Los Angeles: Semiotext(e), 2012.

Watson, Don. *Gobbledygook: How Clichés, Sludge and Management-Speak Are Strangling Our Public Language*. London: Atlantic, 2004.

Welby, Justin. *Dethroning Mammon*. London: Bloomsbury, 2016.

Westphal, Merold. *Kierkegaard's Critique of Reason and Society*. University Park, PA: Pennsylvania State University Press, 1991.

White, Andrew Dickson. *A History of the Warfare of Science with Theology in Christendom*. Cambridge: Cambridge University Press, 2009.

Wink, Walter. *Engaging the Powers: Discernment and Resistance in a World of Domination*. Minneapolis: Fortress, 1992.

Wood, Diana. *Medieval Economic Thought*. Cambridge: Cambridge University Press, 2002.

Yannaras, Christos. *Against Religion: The Alienation of the Ecclesial Event*. Brookline, MA: Holy Cross Orthodox Press, 2013.

Made in the USA
Coppell, TX
25 July 2022

80411831R00088